FIELDBOOK OF PACIFIC NORTHWEST

SEA CREATURES

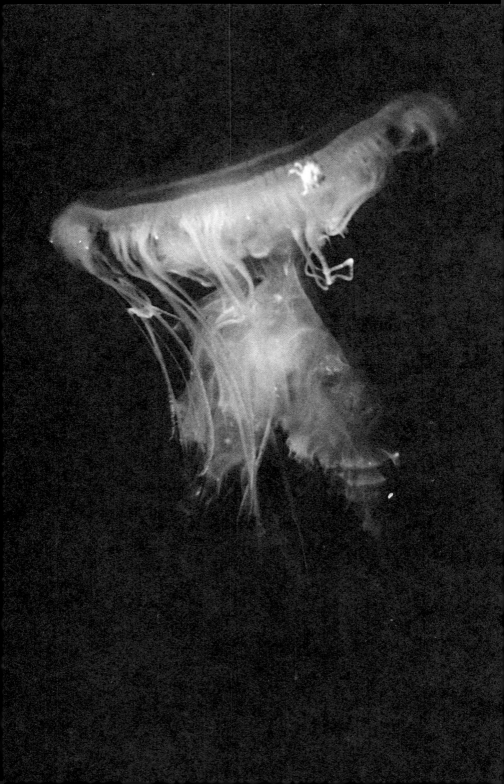

FIELDBOOK OF PACIFIC NORTHWEST

SEA CREATURES

Dan H. McLachlan
Jak Ayres

Naturegraph

Library of Congress Cataloging in Publication Data

McLachlan, Dan H   1942-
    Fieldbook of Pacific Northwest sea creatures.

    Bibliography: p.
    Includes index.
    1. Marine fauna--Northwest, Pacific--Identification.
I. Ayres, Jak, 1947-   joint author.   II. Title.
III. Title: Sea creatures.
QL138.M33   574.92'6'3   79-9769

ISBN   0-87961-068-9   Paper Edition
ISBN   0-87961-069-7   Cloth Edition

Naturegraph Publishers, Inc., Happy Camp, CA 96039

To our families, our friends, and to the preservation of the oceans.

ACKNOWLEDGMENTS

We would like to acknowledge the help given by the following people: Bob Combo of the Washington State Department of Fisheries in Olympia, Don Bloye, Mike Kyte, Tony Lucas, Neil Herd, Pat Siedlak, Dave Columbus, Peter C. Howorth, William L. High, Judy Wagner, Bob Turner, and Larry Martin for their photographs; Tom Suchanek, Ken Sebens, and Gary Laakso of the University of Washington, and Larry Moulton and Ken Conte for photographs and hours of help. We also thank: Lois Ayres, Di and Peter McLachlan for their help and love; Mark Helland and Jim Gaudette for valued assistance; Jane Howorth for her abalone and shark drawings; Bob Jowett and Earl Ewing of the *Tacoma News Tribune* for their skills at color separation work; and our other friends who gave their support and encouragement.

Finally, we are deeply indebted to three people: Dr. Ron Shimek, Assistant Professor of Zoology, University of Alaska at Anchorage for providing photographs and for being one of the book's chief technical consultants in matters of biology; Chris Nelson for her tremendous artistic talents throughout the publication of the book; and our dear friend Sevrin Housen who made this book possible by working endless hours by himself and with the staff at Naturegraph, thereby changing the idea into a reality.

We hope the readers of this book will feel free to help us with slides and advice so that it may be improved. Please address your letters to:

Dan H. McLachlan and Jak Ayres
P. O. Box 1037
Olympia, WA 98507

CONTENTS

CONTENTS BY ANIMAL

INTRODUCTION

Standing ankle deep in the powdered rock of the moon's surface, and in a comtemplative mood looking overhead at the brilliant blue sphere of the earth hanging in the total blackness of the lunar sky, the astronauts must have been gripped by the sudden awareness of how intensely beautiful and precious their distant home really is. And knowing that in the void of space there is only this one, solitary, blue marble, must have made them want to return to warn everyone that it is one of a kind, that there are no others, that it is as fragile as a soap bubble.

The earth's biosphere is seen as a cellophane-thin layer of water and air that supports all life and which makes this planet so unique in the universe. Seventy percent of the biosphere is water, and without this, the rest would not have happened. The majority of all life is produced only in the sunlit top one hundred feet of water along the shorelines. It is within this thin, meandering thread of life that sea stars, octopuses, clams, rockfishes, and most marine creatures are born, feed, procreate, and die.

The Pacific Northwest has one of the richest inland bodies of salt water in the world. Whales, seals, salmon, and a wide variety of other animals either developed here through the ages or have made it their home. It has deep, flowing waters that are constantly fed by glaciers rich with minerals, and only recently have men begun to plow under and pave over its warm, shallow marshes. Also, atomic reactors, substations, oil refineries, steel mills, superports and giant industries and their poisonous wastes are relatively rare here. In short, these cold, pale green waters are America's best and her last.

This book is a family album of the animals which live in the waters of the Pacific Northwest. Their pictures were taken by those of us who have been so overwhelmed by their beauty and their lives that we have not been able to resist studying, reading about, and photographing them. Included are most of the animals a tide-pool gazer or a diver is ever likely to see. We have organized them according to the complexity of their body structures, from simple to more complex, so that the reader will be able to turn to them quickly even under field conditions. They are grouped according to the phyla and classes they belong to, and before each grouping is an explanation as to what the members of each phylum or class share in common and what characteristics they have which set them apart from other animals. Almost every picture was taken of the organism in its natural environment, undisturbed. Along with each picture is an explanation of the animal's particular traits, habits and eccentricities, with an emphasis on the prime concept that in nature, every change, action, or interaction has consequences.

As educators, photographers and conservationists, we have learned that once people can place a name to what they are seeing and can understand its importance to the earth, it becomes natural for them to want to enjoy and protect it. Men do not set aside wildlife refuges out of ignorance, but out of understanding. The man who is awe struck by the sight of whales dozing in a quiet cove, or by the precise turnings of clouds of waterfowl over a delta, is the man of learning and grateful heart.

We favor leaving animal and plant life unharmed in their natural environments. Though we realize that certain numbers of marine animals must be caught each year for research purposes, we also feel that trappers, foragers, and tide-pool collectors who are not scientists actively involved in doing research, are creating, by their sheer numbers, a real ecological threat to the intertidal environment. And therefore, we would like to encourage people to be careful where they place their feet, to turn back overturned rocks, and to leave unharmed all creatures so that they might continue to live in natural, unspoiled ways.

The earth will survive man, its most predatory of all creatures, only when people understand that this planet is a tiny, fragile speck of blue that is whirling through the empty, totally cold, blackness of space; that the forms of life clinging to its surface are there together as a family breathing the same air, drinking the same water, with the oceans in their veins; and that when any of their members is driven to extinction it is *lost forever* to the universe—an act that constitutes the most unforgivable, most unthinkable of crimes.

FIELD KEY

When you find something in a tide pool, on the beach or while diving, that you do not know the name of, you may either look through the pictures in this book until you recognize it, or you may first use this simplified field key. Through simple, naked-eye observations, this key will direct you to determine what phylum, and in most cases which class, the animal you are studying belongs to. (See Contents for the page numbers of the different phyla and classes.) If what you have found is an uncommon animal and not included in this fieldbook, this key will at least help you find it in more specialized texts.

---

1.   If it has no definite body plan and is encrusting surfaces in lumpy or spongy patches, go on to 2.

   If it has a definite body plan, go on to 3.

---

2.   If it has numerous pores or one large opening and many small pores, is spongy or feltlike, and is encrusting or lumpy, it belongs to the phylum Porifera.

   If it grows in brittle encrusting patches or lichenlike groupings and is made up of tiny boxlike structures, it belongs to the phylum Bryozoa.

   If it has many pores and is lumpy with a jellylike covering, it belongs to the phylum Chordata and the class Ascidiacea.

---

3.   If it has radial symmetry go on to 4.

   If it has bilateral symmetry go on to 9.

---

4.   If it is a soft, featherlike animal covered with polyps with tentacles, it belongs to the phylum Cnidaria and the class Hydrozoa.

   If it is a hard, bushylike growth made up of boxlike structures, it belongs to the phylum Bryozoa.

   If it is attached as an individual, go to 5.

   If it is free-moving, go to 6.

---

5.   If it is vaselike with a single large opening and has many pores along its body, it belongs to the phylum Porifera.

If it is stalked or attached by the base, has two openings and its color falls in the range from transparent to red, brown, orange, or pink, it belongs to the phylum Chordata and the class Ascidiacea.

If it is flowerlike, has a column and has tentacles around an opening, it belongs to the phylum Cnidaria and the class Anthozoa.

If it is volcanolike in structure, is white or off-white, or is stalked with several white plates, it belongs to the phylum Arthropoda and the class Crustacea.

6.   If it is star-shaped, cucumber-shaped or oval, has tube feet, spines or is soft-bodied, it belongs to the phylum Echinodermata. Go to 7 for the class it belongs to.

If it is swimming or floating, go to 8.

7.   If it has five to twenty arms which are not jointed and is slow-moving with tube feet on its ventral side, it belongs to the class Asteroidea.

If it has five flexible arms (occasionally branched) and is perhaps fast-moving, it belongs to the class Ophiuroidea.

If it has spines (perhaps tiny) covering its body, and its mouth is on its ventral side, it belongs to the class Echinoidea.

If it falls into the color range from red to white and is shaped like a cucumber with bushy tentacles emerging from its substrate, it belongs to the class Holothuroidea.

8.   If it is a jellyfish with tentacles near its margin and its mouth has no lobes, it belongs to the phylum Cnidaria, class Hydrozoa.

If it is a translucent, yellow, white or pink jellyfish with tentacles near the margin, has a mouth with long lobes, and is perhaps larger than four inches (10 cm), it belongs to the phylum Cnidaria, class Scyphozoa.

If it is a jellyfish with a globe-shaped body and its tentacles (if present) are two in number and branched, it belongs to the phylum Ctenophora.

9.   If it is wormlike or a tube with a feathery structure extending from it, go to 10.

If it is not wormlike, go to 11.

---

10. If it is flat-bodied or perhaps looks globulous, and moves in a gliding motion, it belongs to the phylum Platyhelminthes.

If it is threadlike or ribbonlike with no segments, is easily broken, and is seen free-swimming or among rocks or sand, it belongs to the phylum Nemertea.

If it is a segmented worm found in the sand, in mussel beds, on pilings or under rocks, or if it has formed protective tubes for itself from parchmentlike material, bits of substrate, or calcareous material (from which feathery gills may project), it belongs to the phylum Annelida.

---

11. If it has a shell, plates, or is sluglike, it belongs to the diverse phylum Mollusca to which clams, oysters, chitons, limpets, snails, nudi-branchs, octopuses, and squids all belong. To determine its class, go to 12.

If it is clamlike with two shells and is attached by a stalk, it belongs to the phylum Brachiopoda.

If it has a stiff or shell-like body covering with jointed appendages, it belongs to the phylum Arthropoda.

If it is fishlike, it belongs to the phylum Chordata. Go to 13 to determine its class.

---

12. If it is oval-shaped with eight plates and a large ventral foot, it belongs to the class Amphineura.

If it has a coiled or cone-shaped shell, or if it is sluglike, it belongs to the class Gastropoda.

If it has two shells, it belongs to the class Bivalvia.

If it has eight or ten tentacles and two eyes, it belongs to the class Cephalopoda.

---

13. If it is a fish with a breathing spiracle or more than one pair of gill slits, it belongs to the class Chondrichthyes.

If it is a fish with only one pair of gill slits, it belongs to the class Osteichthyes.

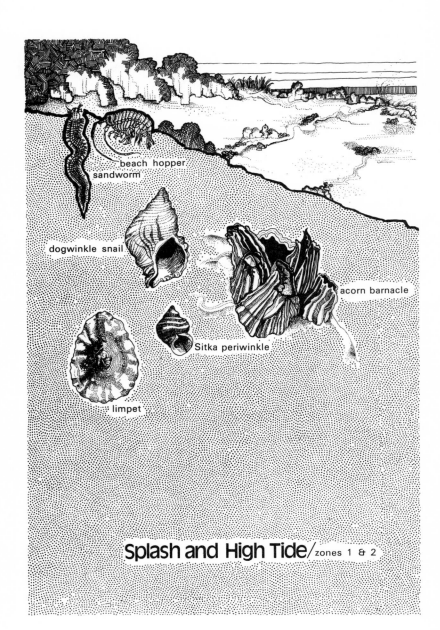

beach hopper
sandworm

dogwinkle snail

acorn barnacle

Sitka periwinkle

limpet

Splash and High Tide/zones 1 & 2

THE ZONES

A few years ago marine animal field studies were done almost exclusively in the intertidal zones. Today, with the recent availability of the self-contained underwater breathing apparatus known as SCUBA, this has changed. An increasing number of marine scientists are learning to use the new equipment and are entering the subtidal world to view it for the first time, really, as one of its own. In other words, the scientist has become like a fish himself, and the limited view of the tidal world has been expanded to encompass the world of the deep.

Nevertheless, the majority of people do not have access to such sophisticated equipment and so must rely on the tide pools and shores to provide clues for understanding the greater marine world. Where then, and at what stages of the tides, may one find those animals discussed in the following pages?

ZONE ONE

If the animal described is categorized by a number 1, it may be found in the *splash zone*, that part of the shore where only the spray of breaking waves reaches.

ZONE TWO

If the animal is a number 2, it is found in the *high tide zone*, that part of the shore covered only when the waters are at their fullest tide, which may last for no more than one to four hours at a time.

ZONE THREE

If the animal is a number 3, it is found in that portion of the shore that is under water about as much of the time as it is out of water. This is the *middle tide zone.*

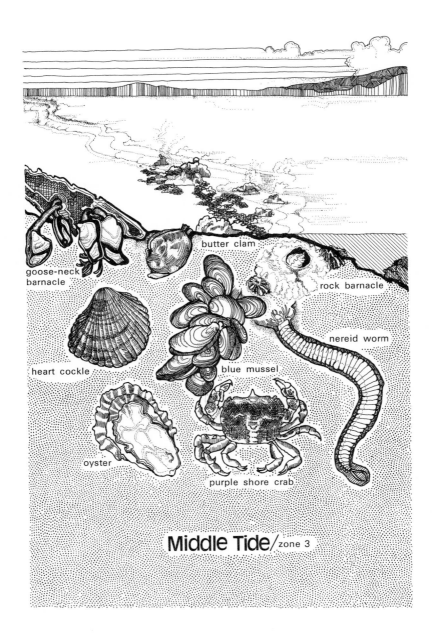

goose-neck
barnacle

butter clam

rock barnacle

nereid worm

heart cockle

blue mussel

oyster

purple shore crab

Middle Tide/zone 3

ZONE FOUR

If the animal is a number 4, it may be found during the one to four hours when the waters are at their very lowest. This is the *low tide zone.*

ZONE FIVE

If the animal is categorized by a number 5, it is considered to be a *subtidal* creature, or one that remains below the lowest reaches of the tides. To see these creatures one must look into the tide pools at low tide in hopes of spotting them there in the shallow waters. Occasionally subtidal creatures are trapped in such tide pools or have taken up permanent residence in them despite the dangers inherent during those hours when their homes are cut off from deeper waters.

What one must remember is that very few animals found living in the intertidal zones are actually *thriving* there. The majority are simply toughing it out and trying to keep moist until the waters return. Some, such as shore crabs, hide under rocks in the dark, wet gravel; others, such as limpets, clams, mussels and barnacles, enclose themselves within ingeniously designed shells.

Why, then, are they there at all? In the case of certain barnacles and mussels, it is because they need a great deal of water movement to bring them a supply of food, and the waves of the intertidal zones fulfill that need. Others have adapted to this outer edge of the marine world either to take advantage of food supplies other animals cannot reach, or to escape an overpopulated or excessively competitive subtidal environment. Still others have adapted to the intertidal zone to escape the attacks of persistent subtidal predators. The oysters in Hood Canal are a clear example of the latter, for within recent years a growing sea star population has so decimated their numbers that the only survivors are those that are growing in the intertidal zones beyond the sea stars' reach.

For many creatures, the move from the subtidal world into the intertidal world was a leap from the frying pan into the fire. For them, the new problems have come from climactic temperature changes, mudslides and shifting beaches, and from biological factors such as predation from birds and human beings. Presently, their worst threat comes from pollutants and oil spills because pollutants and oil spills mean death for nearly every intertidal creature they touch. Oil, whether it is thin kerosene or the thick tarlike type, entraps, smothers, and chemically burns intertidal creatures. It is no wonder that this threat to the survival of sea creatures is one of the greatest concerns of marine biologists today.

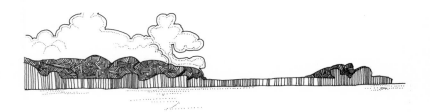

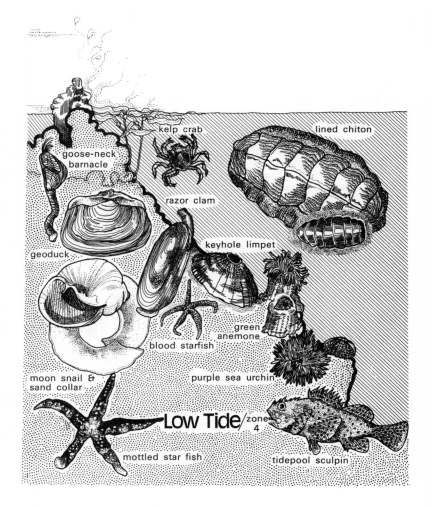

kelp crab

lined chiton

goose-neck
barnacle

razor clam

keyhole limpet

geoduck

green
anemone

blood starfish

moon snail &
sand collar

purple sea urchin

Low Tide/zone 4

mottled star fish

tidepool sculpin

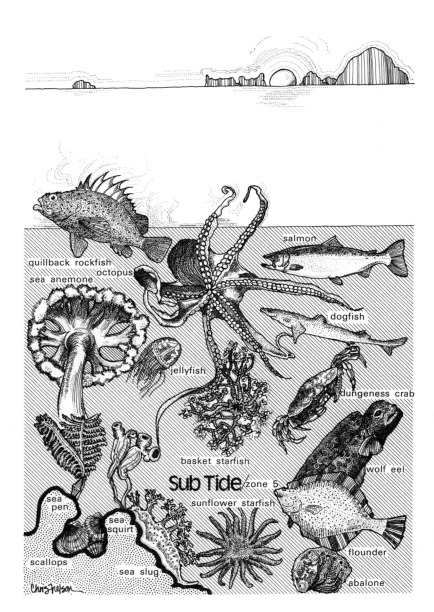

quillback rockfish

sea anemone

octopus

salmon

dogfish

jellyfish

dungeness crab

basket starfish

Sub Tide/zone 5

sea pen

sea squirt

sunflower starfish

wolf eel

flounder

scallops

sea slug

abalone

1

PORIFERA: the Sponges
classes: Calcarea, Hyalospongia, Demospongiae

The one-celled plants and animals on this planet are the simplest. They are the "soup" that supports the rest of life. Together, they form the foundation of plankton without which all animals in the oceans would perish. Plankton are also responsible for manufacturing seventy percent of the world's oxygen. Their importance to life on this planet is therefore quite apparent, even though they are so tiny as individuals that they are invisible to the naked eye.

One-celled plants are called protophyta; one-celled animals, protozoa. Protozoa are capable of digestion, respiration, movement, and reproduction. They function as individuals or in colonies. Some are capable of luminescence and, when the bow of a boat, a wave, or a swimmer's movement agitates them at night, will light up summer waters with a ghostly blue light filled with bright sparks.

Multicelled animals are called metazoa. All animals that are not protozoa fall into this group. The simplest forms of animal life that are multicelled are the sponges, which form the phylum Porifera. Sponges are so simple, in fact, that for many centuries people debated whether or not they were animals at all and not plants. After men like Aristotle helped establish them as animals, the debate was whether or not they were colonies of protozoa or multicelled animals, metazoa. The development of improved microscopes finally proved sponges to be extremely simple multicellular animals with cells that perform specialized interdependent functions.

All but one kind of sponge live in salt water. Most prefer shallow waters. Some cling to rocks as plants do; others encrust rocks, appearing like a porous layer of flesh; and still others live on the valves of pectens or provide homes for a type of hermit crab that burrows into them and carries them. With the pectens and hermit crabs, sponges have a commensal relationship. That is, they live and eat together. Sponges and pectens do not have a parasitic relationship (in which one feeds on the other), but a symbiotic one (one helps the other), for the sponge provides a surface too rough for the pecten's enemy, the sea star, to get a grip on.

The Pacific Northwest boasts just short of one hundred species of sponges, while over two thousand five hundred different species have been identified throughout the world. These animals come in an almost unlimited number of shapes and sizes, ranging in color from black to violet, red, brown, green, and yellow. Because of this diversity and their simplicity, identification with the naked eye, from a practical standpoint, is impossible. Some species, however, are conspicuous enough to be identified by the observer. We have included photographs of a number of these (see pp. 33-36).

The surfaces of sponges are covered with fine pores called ostia, and larger pores that look like miniature volcanoes, oscula. Sponges draw water into their incurrent canals through the small pores which strain out the larger debris. They excrete used water out the larger pores. Water, once inside a sponge, flows from the incurrent canals into ciliated chambers. These chambers, or cavities, are lined with cells called choanocytes. Each choanocyte has a fine hair (flagellum) extending from it. The flagella create a current that carries water through the sponge while the cells absorb oxygen and feed on plankton, which are drawn in through a collared opening at the base of each flagellum.

There are three classes of sponges, Calcarea, Hyalospongia, and Demospongiae. Classifications are based on what material the sponges

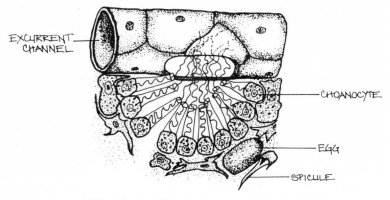

BASIC INTERNAL ANATOMY OF THE SPONGE

use for their skeletal support. Calcarea have hard calcareous spicules to support them and give them shape. Noncalcareous sponges (Hyalospongia and Demospongiae) get their support from either flexible spongin fiber, siliceous spicules, or a combination of both. Spicules are made of silica or carbonate of lime, and look like tiny needles, anchors, maces, spears, arrows, jacks, grappling hooks, not to mention a wide variety of other shapes. Noncalcareous sponges are identified further by examining the shapes of the spicules. Every species has its own unique combination of shapes. Some very delicate sponges are almost entirely supported by spicules. Bath sponges are predominately made up of spongin.

Though various animals will burrow into sponges and make them their hiding places, they do not eat them per se. The spiny spicules and unpleasant taste of sponges leave them relatively free from many predators, but not from people, nudibranchs, or the slime sea star. Before synthetic sponges became popular, sponge gatherers wiped out large areas of sponges the world over. Now sponge farming has been found possible. By a special procedure, a single sponge can be diced into tiny fragments and successfully replanted to grow into as many new sponges as there are pieces. This has to be done with care, however, for if a sponge is exposed to the air, the air may enter its pores and kill it.

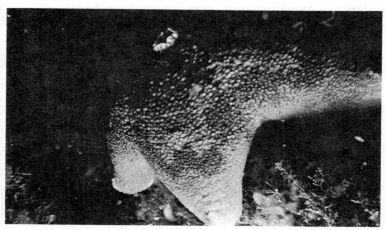

slime star, *Pteraster tesselatus* Sponge predator *(Photo by Dan H. McLachlan)*

The relative independence of sponge cells illustrated by this ability to regenerate from tiny "cuttings" accounts for the method some sponges use to reproduce. These sponges simply constrict themselves towards the ends of their branches until the branch ends fall off and attach themselves to the substrate to regenerate into new individuals. This asexual method of reproduction is called budding. Another unusual method for sponges to reproduce, though more common among fresh water sponges that must endure drought and freezing conditions during long winter months, is to surround food enriched cells with a tough, protective coating made up of spicules and connective cells. The resulting egglike structures are called gemmules, and they can survive the elements long after the parent sponge has disintegrated.

Both hermaphroditic (producing both sperm and eggs) and dioecious (producing only sperm or eggs) species of sponges exist. Sperm cells and egg cells develop spontaneously within the sponge walls from transformed sponge cells. The sperm cells then enter the excurrent water columns and leave the sponge through the oscula and enter other sponges through their ostia and incurrent water columns. Once inside the flagellated chambers they are carried by specialized cells to the eggs which still rest within the tissue of the sponge walls. After fertilization, the resulting embryos develop within the body wall until they reach the larval stage, at which point they break out and are carried by the excurrent water to the open. After a short, free-swimming existence, the sponge larvae settle and attach themselves to desired surfaces, then grow into adult sponges.

Presently, the greatest threat to the sponge is pollution. Insecticides, radioactive wastes and other man-made pollutants are threatening to kill off the levels of plankton upon which sponges (and all life on this planet, for that matter) depend. For this reason, sponges can provide a gauge of environmental quality. When sponges begin to die, people must become concerned.

crumb-of-bread sponge, *Halichondria panicea* The crumb-of-bread sponge varies in color and form. Although green in the photo above, it is often tan or yellow. About one-half inch (1-2 cm) thick, *Halichondria* may be found encrusting floats, pilings or rocks. It has many raised oscula (excurrent pores) scattered over its surface, and a texture like bread. *(Photo by Thomas H. Suchanek)* zones 4 , 5

purple encrusting sponge, *Haliclona permollis* Gray to violet, the purple encrusting sponge is one inch (2.5 cm) thick and forms extensive patches on floats, rocks, and pilings. Its large cone-shaped oscula are seemingly random in their arrangement among the smaller incurrent pores. *(Photo by Thomas H. Suchanek)* zone 4

smooth pecten sponge, *Mycale adhaerens*   The smooth pecten sponge commonly grows on valves of pecten scallops *(Chlamys)*. The small oscula give it a smoother texture than the large-pored rough pecten sponge. It is soft to the touch and yellow, brown, or violet. *(Photo by Don Bloye)*   zone   5

rough pecten sponge, *Myxilla incrustans*   The coarse-looking rough pecten sponge is usually found encrusting the upper valves of *Chlamys*. Its oscula may reach one-fourth inch (6 mm) in diameter. In many ways similar to the smooth pecten sponge, it also feels soft and appears yellow to brown. *(Photo by Bob Turner)*   zone   5

boring sponge, *Cliona celata* Boring sponges are commonly found in the valves of rock scallops, oysters, and in the cracks of rocks. They appear as thin lines of yellow dots. By a chemical process they etch out portions of marine shells, creating a habitat for themselves as well as serving as decomposers. *(Photo by Dan H. McLachlan)* zone 5

dead man's fingers, *Syringella amphispicula* Brightly colored in yellow, red, or lavender, dead man's fingers is a large erect sponge that grows up to eight inches (20.5 cm) high. It may occur in great concentrations. *(Photo by Ronald L. Shimek)* zone 5

cloud sponge, *Aphrocallistes vastus*   The cloud sponge may be small or may grow as large as four feet. It may be shaped like a trumpet, a cloud, or like fingers, and provides protective shelter for many sea creatures. *(Photo by Don Bloye)*   zone   5

calcareous sponge, *Scypha*   This rather uncommon sponge belongs to the class Calcarea. It can be found attached by the base to rocks or pilings. Its most unusual characteristic is its one large osculum which makes it resemble a sea squirt (ascidian). *(Photo by Dan H. McLachlan)*   zone   5

2.

CNIDARIA: the Jellyfishes and Polyplike Animals

The animals that share a common level of growing complexity just above that of the sponges, the Porifera, belong to the phylum Cnidaria. They include such animals as jellyfishes, sea anemones, sea pens, and the plantlike hydroids.

Cnidarians were named coelenterates back in the days when people were debating whether or not poriferans were plants or animals, and coelenterates were called zoophytes which indicated that they were half plant, half animal. Now they are known to be animals and not plants, and cnidarians are commonly referred to simply as polyps.

Several things make cnidarians more complex than poriferans. For one thing, they have a true mouth into which they take food and from which they excrete waste. Secondly, they have a digestive cavity, and though it is no more than just a sac, it does the job. They also have a primitive sort of nervous system, which, though it has no central control, is capable of performing some rather complex jobs for the animal. Finally, cnidarians are not built haphazardly, but with design.

Cnidarians are designed radially. The internal sac is shaped around an imaginary axis and partitions radiate out from the sac's lining to the outer skin, so that a number of divisions are formed in the mesogloea (middle jelly). Tentacles also radiate around the mouths of cnidarians and are armed with tiny stinging cells called nematocysts. Nematocysts can be present on the outer skin of the cnidarians too. The poisonous barbs and looped hairs of the nematocysts allow the tentacles to draw food into the mouth of the animal. If small fishes, shrimps, or other such creatures happen to brush up against the often quite long and well-camouflaged tentacles, they are quickly subdued by the paralyzing effects of the nematocysts, which are triggered to dart out at them upon touch. Since cnidarians are meat eaters, they are classified as carnivores.

Some cnidarians form colonies. Their cells communicate functions; and their tasks, as we will describe in the following sections, are often very specialized and quite unusual. The three classes in the phylum Cnidaria are Hydrozoa, Scyphozoa, and Anthozoa.

CNIDARIA: class Hydrozoa

One can understand how hydroids were once mistaken for plants because they look like dusty ferns growing from the ocean's bottom. But when a magnifying glass is held up to their feathery branches, a person can notice that there are little polyps clustered along their stems. In fact, if one looks carefully, he can see the motions of the microscopic tentacles moving back and forth in the water in constant search of food.   These feeding polyps are called zoöids.   They pass the nutrition to other zoöids and parts of the animal via small canals which run the length of the stalks they are attached to.

Not all zoöids are food gatherers. Some are responsible for reproduction and create miniature jellyfishes called medusae, which they release like transparent flying saucers to start new hydroid colonies elsewhere. When these free-swimming medusae are sufficiently matured many months later, they lay eggs that develop into larvae called planulae. These in turn grow into new hydroids. The entire cycle may take a full year to complete.

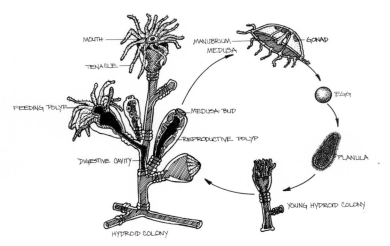

THE REPRODUCTIVE CYCLE OF HYDROZOANS,
ALTERNATION OF GENERATIONS

This type of reproduction, called alternation of generations (or metagenesis), is very unusual in the animal kingdom and has been the subject of much study in the past. But certain other hydroids reproduce without this metamorphosis.   For some, only the medusoid stage is known, and rather than laying eggs that develop into polyps, they develop into another generation of medusae. Still other hydroids have taken to floating unattached in the ocean waters and grow in colonies by budding, with reproduction being done by specialized individuals which produce either sperm or eggs.   Among the most sinister of these latter types is the deadly Portuguese man-of-war, which floats on the surface of the world's tropical oceans suspended from a balloon-like bladder of air.   It is the Portuguese man-of-war, with its long, trailing cords of nematocyst-armed tentacles, that swimmers have good reason to fear.   Severely entangled swimmers have died from shock after encountering them.

ostrich plume hydroid, *Aglaophenia*   The well-named ostrich plume hydroid appears in clusters with brownish plumes up to six inches (15 cm) in length. This hydroid doesn't have a medusoid stage. Reproductive structures, called corbulae, contain the polyps that develop into the larvae which escape to settle and start new colonies. *(Photo by Dan H. McLachlan)*   zone 5

water jellyfish, *Aequorea aequorea*   The water jellyfish has a colorless, jellolike disc two inches (5 cm) in diameter and is three or four times broader than high. Numerous white lines, called radial canals, radiate from the center of this hydroid and transport food through its body. When disturbed at night, the water jellyfish will give off a soft biolumin-escence. *(Photo by Dan H. McLachlan)*   zone 5

pink-mouthed hydroids, *Tubularia* The pink-mouthed hydroids are spectacular polyps that unfold atop branchless stalks up to three inches (7 cm) high. Two sets of tentacles surround their mouths. The medusoid stage stays in close contact with the "mother" polyp, and it will not leave until ready to form the hydroid stage. *Tubularia* develops in clusters and appears like small bushy debris on floats, boats, and rocks. *(Photo by Kenneth P. Sebens)* zones 4 , 5

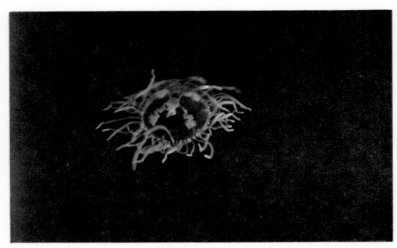

orange-striped jellyfish, *Gonionemus vertens*   This medusa comes from a tiny solitary hydroid. With a diameter of about half an inch (1.2 cm), it can be noticed hanging among eelgrass and kelps. The long tentacles have adhesive pads for clinging. The bell has an orange or brown cast to it, and the gonads lie along the radial canals. It eats crustaceans and swimming larvae. *(Photo by Ken Conte)*   zone   5

purple sail jellyfish, *Velella velella*   A beautiful blue colonial hydroid, the purple sail jelly-fish looks like a tiny bubble with a transparent paper sail, and they are also widely known as "by-the-wind sailors." The authors have seen them offshore in great masses, stretching from horizon to horizon. Individual stinging polyps are attached to the underside from a central feeding polyp. Sometimes seen washed up on shore, they are up to three or four inches (8-10 cm) in diameter. *(Photo by Thomas H. Suchanek)*   zone   5

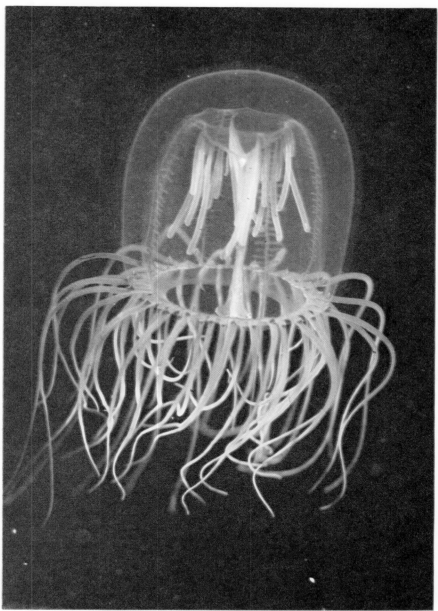

red-eyed jellyfish, *Polyorchis penicillatus*   The nearly transparent red-eyed jellyfish is
bell-shaped. Its internal organs, which can be plainly seen, are fingerlike. A graceful
pulsing motion propels it through the water. Heavy tentacles lace the margin of the bell
which is one to two inches (2-5 cm) in diameter. Bright red spots are situated in a row at
the base of the tentacles. *(Photo by William L. High)*   zone   5

CNIDARIA: class Scyphozoa

What most people call "jellyfish" fall into two classes, Hydrozoa (covered in the preceding section) and Scyphozoa. The scyphozoan medusae (jellyfishes) never come from hydroids. Telling scyphozoan medusae and hydrozoan medusae apart can be a difficult chore because even though their life cycles are different, structurally they are very similar. One feature that does distinguish the scyphozoan medusae rather well, however, is the presence of their gonads just off to the sides of their body cavities, rather than out on the radial canals as with hydrozoan medusae. The gonads are detectable as having more coloration generally than the rest of the umbrella-shaped mantles of the jellyfishes.

Jellyfishes are not fishes; they are much too primitive to qualify. In the Pacific Northwest, they range from the size of a grain of rice to three feet (.9 m) in diameter, and in certain parts of the world they are reported to grow as large as eight feet (2.4 m) in diameter. No known species lives longer than a year, and it is not an uncommon sight to see beaches littered with their carcasses. Fortunately they are ninety-nine percent water and soon decompose into the sand.

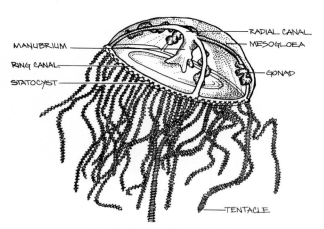

ANATOMY OF SCYPHOMEDUSA

Another odd thing about jellyfishes (both hydrozoans and scypho-zoans) is that many luminesce to a certain degree. Hydrozoan medusae *Aequorea* are particularly good at this and, when touched on a dark night, look like pale blue flying saucers with their running lights turned on. For those people who like to walk beaches on late summer nights, and for scuba divers who brave the blackness, this jellyfish provides a pleasant diversion. The spots of luminescence that are on the outer margins of the mantles are linked to a system of nerve fibers and provide a very limited source of sensory information.

Like other members in the phylum Cnidaria, jellyfishes are carni-vorous. They collect their prey with tentacles which hang from the margins of their mantles and which are armed with nematocysts. Their nematocysts are quite powerful and as soon as they are touched para-lyze and stun the prey. The tentacles then lift the victim to the mouth to be ingested.

The mouth and stomach of the jellyfish hang from the center of the mantle like a mushroom stalk. This is called the manubrium; after food has been digested within it, the nutrients pass to other parts of the jellyfish along canals which radiate through the mantle.

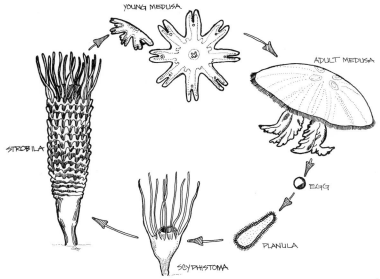

REPRODUCTIVE CYCLE OF SCYPHOZOANS

Sexual reproduction also occurs within the manubrium.   The eggs and sperm drop from the nearby gonads into the body cavity, and later they are expelled from the mouth as cilliated spheres (planulae).   After being released, planulae swim about for a time until they have found suitable objects to attach themselves to.   The planulae then grow into what are called scyphistomae, which look like miniature anemones.   These in turn divide until they look like stacks of tiny, upside down jellyfishes, called strobila.   Later, the strobila will divide up (each) into several individuals that will then mature into scyphozoan medusae.   But not all scyphozoan jellyfishes go through this stage.   With some species, as explained on Hydrozoa (page 38), the young are released from the parent as eggs which develop into miniature medusae; however, it should be pointed out that in the Pacific Northwest this is more the exception than the rule (Kozloff 1974).

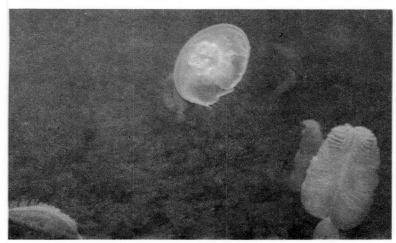

moon jellyfish, *Aurelia aurita*   This disc-shaped, gelatinous animal has four horseshoe-shaped gonads that appear pink in the male and yellow in the female. It begins life as a tiny hydroid attached to the sea floor. They are known to occur in swarms, and their nematocysts may cause discomfort to people. The moon jellyfish is usually five inches (13 cm) in diameter. *(Photo by Dave Columbus)*   zone 5

sea blubber jellyfish, *Cyanea capillata*   The large sea blubber can grow up to seven feet (2.1 m). This jellyfish varies in color from orange to brown. It has a nearly flat umbrella and, beneath, a cleft with eight clusters of long tentacle threads. Although stinging cells line the tentacles, some species of small fish may take refuge among them. *(Photo by Don Bloye)*   zone 5

CNIDARIA: class Anthozoa

Sea anemones and jellyfishes are so similar that anemones can almost be considered jellyfishes that have decided to stand on their heads and take up the sedentary life for a while. Jellyfishes and anemones have the same wall structure; they both use stinging tentacles to gather food; and they both have feeding cavities, though in the case of anemones this cavity is empty of the jelly (mesogloea) that gives the jellyfish its firmness.

The nematocysts of some anemones are so well-developed that they can snare sea creatures as large as shrimps and small fishes. In the Pacific Northwest the anemones do not have tentacles harmful to man; however, the child who puts his tongue to one is in for a nasty surprise.

The structure of an anemone is simple. It attaches itself to rocks, pilings, and discarded junk on the ocean floor by means of a pedal disc. From this a soft inner wall and tougher outer wall extend upwards as a cylinder for as much as three feet (.9 m). At the top, a small, round mouth is located in the center of the enclosure, and around the outer edge of this are the tentacles.   Unlike jellyfishes, the anemone can

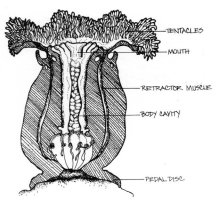

ANATOMY OF A SEA ANEMONE

withdraw its tentacles and mouth into itself and pull its entire length out of harm and into a compact ball. A strong current or the simple touch of a foreign object will trigger this reaction. Some anemones can also move from danger, and, in the case of *Stomphia*, can twist back and forth to swim awkwardly away.

The favorite anemones of underwater photographers are the burrowing anemone, *Pachycerianthus fimbriatus*—with its long, delicate tentacles and an ability to rapidly duck out of sight into its burrows in the sand—and the enormous white- and orange-plumed sun anemone, *Metridium*, which grow in profusion in many places. Though *Metridium* can be seen from above growing on pilings, the bigger ones are at a greater depth, living on the faces of underwater cliffs and on the hulls of sunken ships. This species may grow as tall as two and a half feet (75 cm), and its tentacles blossom to over a foot (31 cm) in diameter. Rather than having thick tentacles like most anemones, *Metridium* look like giant feather dusters or fluffy palm trees standing on the ocean's bottom. Despite the delicacy of their muzzle-soft bodies, these creatures live free of predators once they have outgrown the appetites of certain nudibranchs and sea stars.

Anemones multiply both sexually and asexually. In sexual reproduction, the eggs and sperm are released into the water through the mouth. In asexual reproduction they may simply divide themselves into two, or may cast off bits of the pedal discs (called pedal laceration), which develop into miniature anemones. Those anemones that prefer the asexual method, such as the thumbnail-sized zoanthids, *Epizoanthus*, are found in tight clusters, often completely smothering boulders and small cliffs as they have off Steamboat Island in southern Puget Sound. Larger *Metridium* prefer the sexual method of reproduction, and they are found scattered far and wide, and at tremendous depths. It is not unusual to find a solitary *Metridium* growing from a single small rock in an otherwise barren landscape.

The single characteristic that seems to unite all anemones is that since they cannot drift about in search of food like their cousins the jellyfishes, they prefer areas where there is current or wave action to bring the nutrients to them. Some tropical sea anemones have a commensal relationship in which "decoy" fishes lure their prey, but the majority of species rely on floating microorganisms for their mainstay, so a continual flow of water is a prerequisite to their survival. They proliferate, then, in compression zones where currents or waves butt up against islands or points of land. For this reason, areas like Cape Flattery, the San Juan Islands, and Deception Pass are ideal habitats for them.

Wherever they may be found, anemones, like alpine flowers, are always pleasing. Their sinister beauty and placid, silent simplicity hold one's interest. And those that have remained beyond the reach of curious hands are always there to enjoy simply going about their business as usual, filling the water with brilliant green, red, orange, and white patches of light.

sun anemone, *Metridium senile*   The sun anemone ranges in color from white to shades of orange and yellow, and is found in magnificent forests on pilings, rocks, and sunken ships. A broad, high column supports the large, flowerlike tentacle clusters. Asexual reproduction (basal fragmentation) explains the grouping of similar sun anemones, while the release of gametes into the sea allows a wide distribution. *(Photo by Dan H. McLachlan)*   zones 4 , 5

Christmas anemone, *Tealia crassicornis*   The striking column of this anemone varies in color and is often brilliant green with red mottling. Commonly found among rock outcroppings and ledges, it is known to live sixty to eighty years. The Christmas anemone grows as tall as it is wide, as large as ten inches (25 cm). *(Photo by Dan H. McLachlan)*   zone   4

beaded anemone, *Tealia coriacea*   As pictured, the beaded anemone may only have the greenish oral disc showing above coarse sand or debris. The reddish column (not shown) has pieces of the debris and sand sticking to the adhesive beads (verrucae). Short, thick tentacles come in regular rows of twelve. The pedal disc is from one to two inches (2.5-5 cm) in diameter. *(Photo by Dan H. McLachlan)*   zone   4

pink-tipped green anemone, *Anthopleura elegantissima*   The pink-tipped green anemone differs from the green anemone by virtue of its pink- to purple-tipped tentacles and its small size of two inches (5 cm). This is the common tide pool anemone seen in colonies attached to rocks. It will use its nematocysts to fight or even kill anemones from other colonies, forming lines of demarcation. *(Photo by Jak Ayres)*   zones   3 , 4

green anemone, *Anthopleura xanthogrammica*   Usually found deeper and more solitary than the pink-tipped green anemone, the green anemone grows up to six inches (15 cm) in diameter. Those found hidden from the sun are likely to be paler than the one shown here. The tentacles, which may have purple or reddish ends, are thick and sticky to the touch because of its nematocysts. *(Photo by Jak Ayres)*   zones   4 , 5

zoanthids, *Epizoanthus scotinus*   Colonies of zoanthids blanket the substrate like walls of tiny flowers. The tentacles are lighter in color than the columns. Most individuals do not exceed an inch (2.5 cm) in height. Through asexual budding they form in clumps, but the animal may also reproduce sexually. *(Photo by Dan H. McLachlan)*   zones 4 , 5

brooding anemone, *Epiactis prolifera*   The common habitat of the small [rarely one inch (2.5 cm) high] brooding anemone is on blades of eelgrass. They come in a variety of greens, reds, browns, blues, or purples. A unique feature involves the brooding of young on the column and pedal disc. These young arise from sexual reproduction rather than from budding. Eggs are fertilized within the digestive cavity and develop into mobile larvae. The larvae then move out the pedal disc where they attach until fully developed. *(Photo by Tony Lucas)*   zones 3 , 4 , 5

tube anemone, *Pachycerianthus fimbriatus*   The tube anemone forms a parchmentlike tube coverd with debris and lined with mucus. The tube may extend over two feet (60 cm). There are two circles of tentacles—a stubby set around the mouth, and long, banded, delicate tentacles which sweep widely for food. When startled, this anemone quickly withdraws into its tube. *(Photo by Dan H. McLachlan)*   zone   5

swimming anemone, *Stomphia coccinea*   The swimming anemone attaches itself to rocks and various junk on the ocean bottom. When approached by predatory sea stars, particularly the leather star, it will let go and swim away, contracting the muscles along its body wall much like a worm. It also uses this method of locomotion to move from an unfavorable food-gathering area. *(Photo by Dan H. McLachlan)*   zone   5

sea pen, *Ptilosarcus gurneyi*   The long, fleshy orange stalk of the sea pen is embedded in sandy or muddy substrates and is supported by a stiff central calcareous stalk. Actually a type of coral, it has minute tentacles around the mouth of each colonial polyp lining the two rows of leaves or feathers. At night these rows of leaves bioluminesce in alternating patterns. Sea pens are plankton feeders and are preyed upon by sea stars and nudibranchs. *(Photo by Don Bloye)*   zone 5

sea whip, *Virgularia*   Sea whips occur in large numbers in various muddy-bottomed areas. These slender white colonies wave in the current in a fantasyland manner. They may be as large as two feet (60 cm) in length. The polyps are on the branchlike structures. The colony itself has an expanded tip that lies buried in the mud. They exhibit biolumines-cence in the night, and feed upon plankton. *(Photo by Dan H. McLachlan)*   zones 4 , 5

cup coral, *Balanophyllia elegans*   Cup coral occurs as a bright orange polyp inside a strong outer wall. It is small and grows to half an inch (1.2 cm) in diameter. The form of the cup is designed to help the movement of foods to the mouth and to protect the animal. This coral looks very much like a small lovely anemone and is often confused as one. *(Photo by Dan H. McLachlan)*   zones 4 , 5

3.

CTENOPHORA: the Comb Jellies

Because of their advanced digestive systems and specialized organs, comb jellies are in a phylum all to themselves. They are named comb jellies for the eight rows of unusually arranged cilia that are grouped like marching columns of soldiers or combs down their sides. These cilia beat rhythmically like oars to slowly propel ctenophores through the water.

A distinguishing feature of the ctenophore sea gooseberry, *Pleurobrachia bachei*, is its two long, trailing tentacles. These tentacles look like ragged feathers. They emit from two tentacle sacs near the top of the animal and extend for as much as twelve times its length, or about seven inches (17.5 cm). The muscular tentacles are covered with glue cells (colloblasts) that secrete an adhesive material to entangle small animals which are then conveyed to the mouth at the lower end of the ctenophore. Its digestive tract consists of a mouth, pharynx, and small digestive canals that carry nutrients to the parts of its body. Undigested wastes pass from its mouth and from excretory pores located at its upper end.

One other unusually well-developed feature of ctenophores is the sense organ used to maintain balance and an upright position. This organ, called a statolith, is made up simply of a small, round lump of calcareous material supported at the ends of sensory cilia and sheltered in a dome where the lines of comb plates terminate at the very top of the ctenophore. As the statolith is acted on by gravitational pull, the sensory cilia are tugged on and react in turn by adjusting the beating of the comb plates until the proper positioning is achieved.

Ctenophores are monoecious (containing both sex organs). Sperm and eggs are passed out through their mouths to be fertilized at random in the open water. Eggs usually hatch directly into ctenophores with a short larval stage and take up a life feeding on minute organisms such as oyster spats and the larvae of molluscs, and small fish.

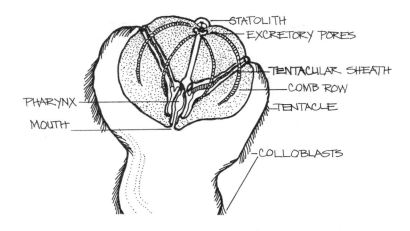

STATOLITH
EXCRETORY PORES
TENTACULAR SHEATH
COMB ROW
TENTACLE
COLLOBLASTS
PHARYNX
MOUTH

ANATOMY OF A CTENOPHORE

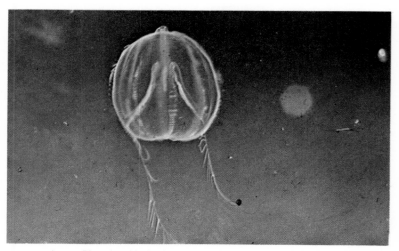

sea gooseberry, *Pleurobrachia bachei* This small, one half inch (1.5 cm) long, egg-shaped ball of jelly is similar in appearance to jellyfishes, but it belongs to a different phylum. On a calm night groups of sea gooseberries may be seen in orange, purple, and green colors. *(Photo by Kenneth P. Sebens)* zone 5

4.

PLATYHELMINTHES: the Flatworms
class: Turbellaria

There is no animal, either on the land or in the sea, that is not a possible carrier of worms—including man. Hookworms, pinworms, tapeworms, bloodworms, liver flukes, and leeches are but a few that have tormented people through the ages. There is no denying it, worms are repulsive. But they do have some saving virtues. If nothing else, one must give them credit for their versatility, for they have what seems to be an almost unlimited capacity for adaptability. Some, for example, accomplish locomotion by attaching themselves to hosts that can provide transportation for them; some drag themselves forward with a telescoping proboscis; some crawl by expanding and contracting their bodies like accordions; and still others swim, propelling themselves with cilia.

Platyhelminthes are the most primitive of the worms, and yet several features place them above the cnidarians. First of all, they have what is called bilateral symmetry, which indicates an equal division can be made in their body structures—a characteristic of higher organisms. They possess definite anterior and posterior ends (heads and tails) and dorsal and ventral sides (top and bottom). Some species also have eyes; and some have sacs containing mineral deposits much like those found in jellyfishes, which act as balance organs.

Flatworms reproduce sexually (they contain both sperm and eggs), and although some smaller species of flatworms are cylindrical in shape, the majority of them are flat and either shaped like leaves or thin tapes.

Unlike more developed worms, Platyhelminthes do not have a circulatory system for carrying nutrient- and oxygen-enriched blood to their cells. Oxygenation takes place by absorbtion through the body walls; and digestion that has been initiated by enzymes created in part by gland cells, is completed intracellularly—within the individual cells. Also, Platyhelminthes do not excrete wastes from an anal opening, for they have but one opening, their mouths, that must serve both ingestive and excretory functions. And finally, Platyhelminthes do not contain their internal organs within a special body cavity as do more developed worms; instead, their organs are simply a part of the tissues of their bodies. All these simple and functional arrangements contribute to this phylum's widespread success at survival.

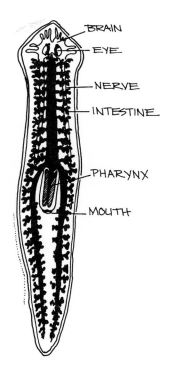

BRAIN

EYE

NERVE

INTESTINE

PHARYNX

MOUTH

ANATOMY OF PLATYHELMINTHES

leaf worm, *Kaburakia excelsa*   Growing up to four inches (10 cm) in length, this is one of the larger flatworms of the Pacific Northwest. Leaf worms are usually dark brown with small dark eye-spots. These eye-spots are simple photocells which receive light. Flatworms are seen among seaweeds, mussel beds, and under rocks. They are carnivores and feed on minute organisms. *(Photo by Jak Ayres)*   zones   4 , 5

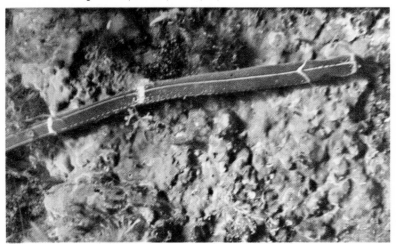

ribbon worm, *Tubulanus sexlineatus*   This large nemertean is about twenty inches (50 cm) long and thinner than a pencil. The ribbon worm has a brownish color with evenly spaced white bands and six longitudinal white lines, one of which runs down the middle of the dorsal side. It is sometimes seen swimming in search of food. *(Photo by Dan H. McLachlan)*   zones   4 , 5

5.

NEMERTEA: the Ribbon Worms

Nemertean worms look like threads or ribbons and are often called such. Charles J. Flora says that he has seen these amazing worms as much as eighty feet long, winding around sponges and coral outcroppings in tropical waters (Flora 1977). Though these worms grow to extraordinary lengths, they are also very fragile and will often simply fall apart at the slightest provocation.

The brittleness of nemerteans is partly for survival reasons. It has been established that if a part as small as the radius is shed, this small part is capable of continued life and will grow into another mature worm. This phenomenon, called autotomy, makes it difficult for a predator to kill an entire threadworm when feeding upon it.

Nemerteans reproduce sexually by randomly releasing sperm and eggs into the water. They have also developed anal openings which places them above the Platyhelminthes. These worms are unique in that they have developed a proboscis (a flexible sensory organ, or "snout"), which has been compared to the finger of a glove that can be turned in and out upon itself. Threadworms use their proboscises both for pulling themselves along (in some cases), and for entrapping and engulfing their prey. These proboscises have sticky substances on their tips or are armed with paralyzing points (thornlike stylets with venom glands attached). When not in use these extensions, which are often long, can be withdrawn until they are needed again.

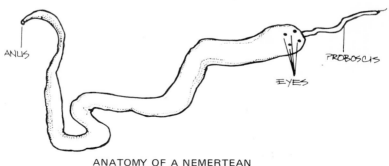

ANATOMY OF A NEMERTEAN

6.

ANNELIDA: the Segmented Worms
classes: Polychaeta, Oligochaeta, Hirudinea

The phylum Annelida contains the segmented worms. The common earthworm, which does so much good by aerating and fertilizing the earth's soil, is of this type. The segmented worms are the most diversified of the worms and therefore the most interesting. Some live in tubes they build in the sand, some in tubes made from seaweeds and mucus, some make parchmentlike tubes that resemble short garden hoses, and still others make hard lime tubes to shelter themselves in. It is also this phylum of worm that has the highly specialized anterior end (head). In some cases these ends have nipper-jaws that resemble the jaws of ants and are used in the same ways. Others have tentacles, bristles, and scales; and some even have tough plates attached, which they can use to seal the ends of their tubes.

Annelids are set apart from the flatworms and threadworms by several features that make them more complex. For one thing, the eyes of several species are well developed. They also have distinct nervous system centers, or ganglia, the largest of which is part of the head and represents the beginnings of a primitive brain. Like all higher animals, they also possess a body cavity (a space between the body organs and the outer wall) that is filled with fluid. Another important fact about annelids is that they have an advanced sort of circulatory system to pump blood. It accomplishes this by contracting the main dorsal and ventral vessels within each segment in a pulsing or continuous peristaltic wave to propel the blood. Some segmented worms have specialized these points of contraction until they have developed into bulbous swellings that can be called hearts because they not only propel the blood, but prevent backflow as well. A further distinguishing feature of annelids, among worms, is that they are segmented or divided into individual units within their body structures.

Annelids reproduce sexually. Like higher animals they are dioecious and therefore contain either the male or female sex organs—though some are monoecious (have both sets of sex organs). They release their eggs and sperm into the water to be fertilized randomly, or wrap their bodies together in a primitive form of coupling. The young have a larval stage, and a few annelids have brood pouches to harbor their young during the early stages of development.

Annelids eat plankton, small animals, seaweeds, and small mud-dwelling organisms, and are therefore considered both carnivorous and herbivorous. They are eaten in turn primarily by fishes, molluscs, and arthropods; consequently they have their place in the ocean's food chain that man depends on so heavily for his food.

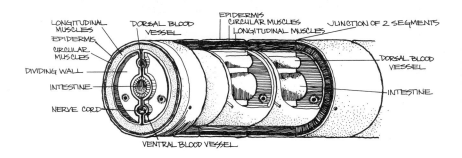

ANATOMY OF AN ANNELID

scale worm, family Polynoidae   Some of these annelids live freely, while some live commensally in the tubes and burrows of other animals. Eighteen overlapping plates on the dorsal surface are a characteristic feature. The scale worm is carnivorous, and will attack and feed on many types of invertebrates, including other worms. The one shown above, *Arctonoe vittata*, was found living with *Diodora*. *(Photo by Jak Ayres)*   zones 3 , 4 , 5

nereid worm, *Nereis*   The common names of some nereids are piling worm, mussel worm, sand worm, and clam worm. They all are obviously segmented, each segment having a pair of parapodia. Colors vary, and they may be three inches (8 cm) in length. The rear segments fill with gametes that are discharged into the open water where fertilization randomly takes place. *(Photo by Jak Ayres)*   zones 3 , 4 , 5

shell binder worm, *Thelepus crispus*   Tubes composed of shell fragments and sand make up the home of the shell binder. This worm may be six inches (15 cm) or more in length. Three pairs of delicate red gills and a semicircle of tentacles gather food and oxygen. The shell binder will relocate if disturbed and quickly build a new tube. It is characterized by its tentacles which appear as many white threads that radiate out over the substrate. *(Photo by Jak Ayres; courtesy of the Seattle Aquarium)*   zone 4

lugworm, *Abarenicola claparedii*   This is one of several lugworms found in the sand and mud of bays and coves. The lugworm burrows into the bottom mudflats, swallowing the mud. It digests the organic material contained, and its wastes are pushed from the burrow, appearing as coils of sand. The muscular contractions by the worms provide the burrows with continuous water movement. This worm is three to six inches (8-15 cm) long. *(Photo by Jak Ayres)*   zones 2 , 3 , 4

plume worm, *Eudistylia vancouveri*   This large worm has beautiful red, green, and blue cirri protruding like feathery plumes from a parchmentlike tube. It is sensitive to the slightest stimuli. Even the shadow of a hand may be picked up by the black eye-spots on the cirri, and the reactions of this worm are as quick as the blink of an eye. Its plumes may be two inches (5 cm) in diameter. Profusions of ten-inch (25 cm) plume worms grow from pilings, sunken ships, and deep fissures in rock. *(Photo by Jak Ayres)*   zones 4 , 5

calcareous tube worm, *Serpula vermicularis*   The calcareous tube worm is seen attached to rocks. While the tube may be long, the animal inside is only two or three inches (5-8 cm) long. The cirri, arranged in two spiraling rows, wave about to snare food and absorb oxygen. When disturbed, this creature withdraws into its tube, closing a flaplike red door (operculum) after it. *(Photo by Dan H. McLachlan)* zones 4 , 5

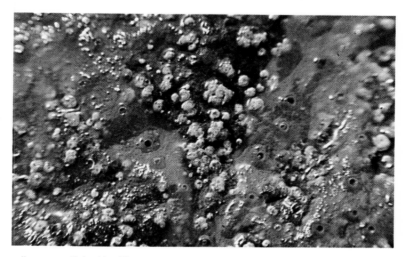

snail worms, *Spirorbis* These tiny red-plumed worms look like miniature feather dusters. The coiled tubes may reach one-fourth inch (6 mm) in diameter. Snail worms live in large populations, and in procreating retain their eggs and brood their young. *(Photo by Jak Ayres)* zones 3 , 4 , 5

bamboo worm, *Axiothella rubrocincta* The brown tube sticking above the mud in this picture shows the home of the bamboo worm. Its tube consists of coarse sand lined with a white parchment. The body is banded bright red. If disturbed, the worm may escape through the lower end of the tube. *(Photo by Jak Ayres)* zones 4 , 5

7

BRYOZOA: the Moss Animals
class: Gymnolaemata

Bryozoa are colonies of microscopic animals. They are difficult animals to identify because there are over two thousand species
world-wide, and to make proper identification, one must use a micro-
scope. The colonies themselves take on a variety of forms, so that
what may look at first glance like a coral, sponge, kelp, jellyfish,
hydroid, or an alga, may in fact be a bryozoan colony. These colonies
may have hundreds of thousands of individuals living in them, and
unlike the hydroids, which are simply interdependent, interconnected
polyps, the individuals within a bryozoan colony, called zoöids, are
much more autonomous, independent, and complete.

Microscopic examination of bryozoans reveals other distinguishing
characteristics. For one thing, zoöids have tentacles like the hydroid
polyps, but instead of being armed with nematocysts, these tentacles
are covered with cilia, which move nutrients into their mouths. Some
species of bryozoans have specialized zoöids, called avicularia, that
look like they have a nipper or "bird's beak" hanging from their tops.
Though these avicularia are constantly opening and closing, they are
not capable of delivering food, so it is assumed they are meant to
ward off trespassers. Some other zoöids, vibracula, have flagellate
filaments that constantly whip the water.

Unlike hydroids, the tentacles which encircle the mouth of a
zoöid (forming what is called the lophophore) can be withdrawn into
the body cavity by a set of muscles, or squeezed out again by another
set of muscles. For added protection, the tops of many zoöids can also
be closed off by a flaplike door, called an operculum. The tentacles,
besides obtaining food for these filter-feeding animals, also provide
them with their sense of touch and carry out respiration. They rely
completely on the water currents to bring nutrients to them. Like
sponges, then, they are a good gauge of changing water quality.

Zoöids each have an esophagus, stomach, and intestine within
their body cavities. The anus is located just off to the side of the

tentacles at the top. As a result, their digestive tracts are U-shaped. The wall of the body cavity is a single layer of cells. The body fluid is a colorless protoplasm which contains white corpuscles. It is the outer covering, zooecium, that the living portion, polypide, secretes. This gives the zoöid its skeletal structure and lends shape to the overall bryozoan colony.

Zoöids have no vascular system (heart, vessels, blood), but they do have a central nerve center (ganglion) and some strands of nerve tissue. They also have an interesting reproductive system which can be either asexual or sexual.

In sexual reproduction, the ripe eggs enter from an egg chamber located directly below the body cavity. Once in the body cavity, they are fertilized by sperm and either released as fertile eggs into the water to grow into larvae, or develop into larvae inside special ovicells that look like large pearls attached to the upper portion of the zoöid. The ciliated larvae, once they have developed, swim about for a time and then attach themselves to suitable surfaces to begin new colonies. The colonies, in turn, grow asexually through budding over the surfaces of rocks and brown algae, and often form beautiful, lacelike patterns more than a foot (30 cm) in diameter.

Bryozoans are everywhere in the ocean. They have been found at the bottom of deep sea trenches as well as in shallow waters. They grow in cracks, under ledges, from the bottom of kelps, and in every other conceivable place. They are master impersonators without trying to be, and because of this, go unnoticed. What is striking about them, however, is the fact that they are, after all, separate, independent individuals that live and thrive successfully as members of a larger, structured community.

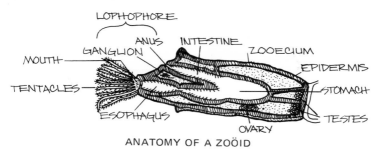

ANATOMY OF A ZOÖID

staghorn bryozoa, *Heteropora magna*   Sometimes mistaken as corals, the staghorn bryozoans have blunt, forked, and rounded branches. Their branches are small, an eighth to a quarter of an inch (3-6 mm) wide, and colonies may be three inches (8 cm) in height. On close examination, the homes of the individuals appear as perforations on the branches. *(Photo by Dan H. McLachlan)*   zone 5

encrusting bryozoa, *Membranipora membranacea*   These animals form flat colonies about one to two inches (2-5 cm) in diameter. Small, white-lined rectangular boxes that contain the individuals radiate symmetrically out from a central point. Often found during summer months on algae, encrusting bryozoans also grow on rocks, glass, and other smooth substrates. *(Photo by Dan H. McLachlan)*   zones 3 , 4 , 5

sea lichen, *Dendrobeania lichenoides*   The pale brown mushroomlike sea lichen may grow to a height and width of one inch (2.5 cm). It occurs on shells, rocks, and on worm tubes, competing for the floating nutrients and a space to attach to. A small stalk is sometimes apparent. *(Photo by Bob Turner)*   zones 3 , 4

snakes head lampshell, *Terebratulina unguicula*   The snakes head lampshell of the phylum Brachiopoda (see following page) is under one inch (2.5 cm) in length, and its shape fits its name well. The shell is a yellowish orange but is usually covered with debris. White clusters of eggs can sometimes be seen on the setae (bristles). *(Photo by Dan H. McLachlan)*   zone 5

8.

BRACHIOPODA: the Lamp Shells

Brachiopods look like living fossils, and since they have been around relatively unchanged for millions of years, they qualify. Outwardly they resemble clams, but rather than being buried in the sand like clams, brachiopods hang from the surfaces of rocks and underwater cliffs by tough, muscular stems, and look like small, brown crabapples. In reality, brachiopods are similar to overgrown zoöids. Brachiopods, like zoöids, gather food with ciliated tentacles; but in the case of a brachiopod, there are two coiled arms, one on each side of the mouth, which, with the help of a thin mucus covering, entrap small microorganisms. These two coils also provide the brachiopod with respiration and limited senses.

The two shells, or valves, of the brachiopod give it protection. The dorsal shell is larger than the ventral shell, and they are held together only by muscles. The tough, flexible stalk that attaches the brachiopod in place emerges through a notch in the upper valve. In order to feed, these two valves must be opened so that water can adequately reach the arms and mouth.

Brachiopods also reproduce very much like bryozoans. Eggs are fertilized within their body cavities (which also contain an esophagus, stomach, and intestine) and are released into the water to develop into free-swimming, ciliated larvae. These larvae have bristly heads and attach themselves to firm surfaces by their posteriors. Once attached, they begin to form the valves from the bottom upwards until they have matured into adult brachiopods.

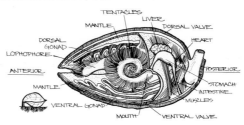

ANATOMY OF A BRACHIOPOD

9.

ECHINODERMATA: the Spiny-skinned Animals
classes: Ophiuroidea and Asteroidea

When a person looks at any creature, he first looks for the head, a pair of eyes, and the mouth. In that way he can organize what he sees in his mind. But when looking at sea stars, sea urchins, sand dollars, and sea cucumbers (members of Echinodermata), this is impossible to do, and as a result, they are the creatures children stand puzzling over at the beach. In fact, they look like nothing from this planet. By stretching the imagination, one could see them as some kind of electrical robots that emit low whirring noises and shuffle about devouring family pets. The shellfish industry would agree that sea stars are nearly that sinister because, along with certain snails, they cause great losses to clam and oyster beds. Not all sea stars feed on shellfish, however. A large percentage feed on organic debris, sponges, sea pens, anemones, fishes, and other sea stars.

The Pacific Northwest has the greatest variety of echinoderms in the world. The sunflower star, *Pycnopodia*, with its twenty or so rays, is also the world's largest and lives only in Northwest waters. The sunflower star, mottled star (*Evasterias*), and pink short-spined star (*Pisaster brevispinus*) are all quite large and very adept at digging up and opening clams and oysters—as many as three a day. They accomplish this by wrapping themselves around the shells and, with the combined suction of thousands of tube feet, easily tugging them open. The stomach membranes which are folded inside the central disc of the stars are then forced out through their mouths onto the tissues of the unfortunate shellfish.

The tube feet of stars are part of a rather remarkable hydraulic system. Through a small madreporite filter located at the center of its rays, the star brings water into a system of internal canals that radiate out the arms to thousands of tiny sacs or bulbs. These bulbs act as reservoirs, and from them water is pushed to and from the tube feet thereby creating the desired amount of suction at their tips. If one remembers that there are tens of thousands of these tube feet, it is easy to understand that the combined suction can exceed one hundred pounds (an estimate). Yet, stars are able to coordinate the function of their tube feet so well that they can glide over the roughest of terrains with effortless fluidity and grace, and can right themselves when placed on their backs. It is remarkable, in light of this, that no echinoderm has a head or brain.

Many sea stars also use their tube feet to dig with. It is not an uncommon sight, among divers, to see large stars at the bottoms of holes—as much as two feet wide and one foot deep—which these creatures dig in pursuit of clams. They accomplish this task quickly and easily by simply remaining stationary over the spot where the clam neck had been protruding from the sand, and by arranging their tube feet to sweep the sand out from under them radially, deftly lowering themselves down. If a star is humped up at the bottom, standing on the tips of its rays, one can assume that it has the clam in its grasp and is feeding on it.

Echinoderms are dioecious, of separate sexes. During the early weeks of summer some species emit eggs and sperm into the cold waters where procreation occurs. The odds are greatly in their favor by virtue of the tremendous quantities involved. When newly developed, the larvae are free-swimming, which allows them to populate far and wide the world over, even to the greatest depths of the oceans.

Echinoderms have two interesting means of protection. First, they have either exposed spines or a compact layer of calcareous plates just under their skins that provide them with armor—hence the name of the phylum, Echinodermata, or spiny-skinned animals. Secondly, sea stars have the amazing ability to rejuvenate parts of their bodies, or even to release arms to predators. Shellfish fishermen learned years ago that to control the sea star population it does no good to chop them up. A star cut in half will more often than not grow back into two stars. Brittle stars and serpent stars, which use their writhing rays rather than their tube feet to propel themselves, will drop a ray upon touch.

Before the introduction of microscopes, how sea stars saw where they were going was a mystery. Actually, they do not have eyes as we think of them, but rather a single, photosensitive cell at the tip of each ray which is only capable of detecting whether or not there is a source of light in the direction the ray is pointed. If a star wishes to move towards the light source, it does so while keeping the ray pointed at it all the while. Also on the end of each ray are the tactile or "touch" tube feet and the olfactory or "smelling" tube feet. These three features are really the "eyes" of the star. With them, the star knows all it needs to about its environment and the food it seeks.

Because the very shape as well as the mobility of echinoderms is dependent on their hydraulic systems, they must be left in the water to be studied or photographed. Out of water they become lifeless, and sea stars and sea cucumbers flatten out like collapsed innertubes. Also, like most other marine creatures, they loose their true coloration within moments of being exposed to air and sunlight. Though the purple and the orange ocre stars are sometimes seen above water on pilings and rocks, this happens only when they are left behind by a tide change.

Echinoderms are enjoyable animals to study and photograph. The basket star is the most unearthly among them, the most photogenic, and the cleverest at gathering food. Built like a tangle of vines, it will shape itself into a makeshift basket using microscopic hooks at the ends of its arms to capture plankton. The vermilion star, blood star, and rose star are the most brightly colored in the Pacific Northwest, while the sun stars are the most varied and colorful.

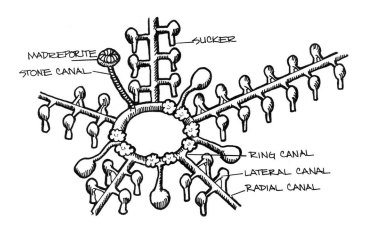

THE HYDRAULICS OF A SEA STAR

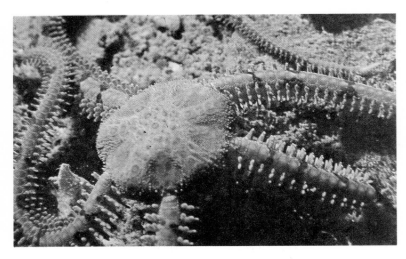

daisy brittle star, *Ophiopholis aculeata*   This common brittle star lives on rocky shores or on kelps, and is found world-wide. It has well-proportioned, black, white, and gray rays (arms) with brown bands. The disc does not exceed one inch (2.5 cm) in diameter. Conspicuous lobes exist on the edge of its disc between the spiny rays. Food passes into the mouth via long flexible tube feet. *(Photo by Michael A. Kyte)*   zones 4 , 5

serpent star, *Amphipholis squamata*   This is the most commonly seen serpent star in the Pacific Northwest and around the world. It is found under rocks intertidally to 100 fathoms. A grazer, it eats algae and detris from the rocks and substrate. *(Photo by Michael A. Kyte)*   zones 4 , 5

basket star, *Gorgonocephalus eucnemis*   Usually deep, ten to one hundred fathoms, this is an exotic-looking brittle star. The arms of this filter feeder develop into hundreds of branchlets that may reach ten to twelve inches (25-30 cm) in diameter. *(Photo by Don Bloye)*   zone   5

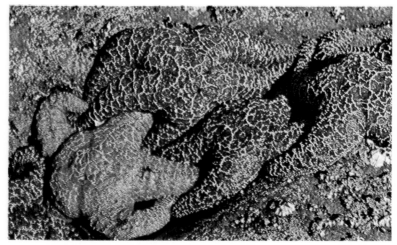

ochre star, *Pisaster ochraceus*   The brightly colored ochre star is often found in groups. It reaches up to twelve inches (30 cm) in diameter, and may be yellow, orange, brown, purple, or pink. This unmistakable star has a thick, broad disc and five somewhat short irregular rays. A skeleton of beadlike calcareous plates gives the body rigidity. At low tide it is, with few exceptions, found in the shade of rocks. *(Photo by Jak Ayres)*   zone   4

pink short-spined star, *Pisaster brevispinus*   One of the largest northwest stars, the pink short-spined star attains a diameter of more than two feet (60 cm). The soft, humped body disc is pink and has five rays. Feeding on other species of sea stars and clams, this star is common in deep water. It will die if exposed to air for more than ten minutes. *(Photo by Dan H. McLachlan)*   zone   5

mottled star, *Evasterias troschelii*   This is a graceful, large one- to two-foot (30-60 cm) star with a small disc and tapering rays. Colors vary from mottled gray, green, orange, or brown, to brick red. The mottled star feeds upon mussels and barnacles that inhabit floats and pilings. *(Photo by Dan H. McLachlan)*   zone   5

six-rayed star, *Leptasterias hexactis*   The small six-rayed star is three inches (8 cm) in diameter. The female carries its eggs in a pouch around her mouth until the young are mature. This sea creature is dull pink to dull green in color, depending on its surroundings. During the brooding period it assumes a humped position and does not eat, but normally it feeds on snails and limpets in eelgrass. *(Photo by Jak Ayres)*   zone   4

sunflower star, *Pycnopodia helianthoides*   The fastest and largest of Northwest sea stars, the sunflower star grows up to three feet (.9 m) in diameter. It is normally orange with violet tufts. The rays break off easily and regenerate. A savage predator, even the lethargic red sea cucumber will gallop away when the sunflower star approaches. *(Photo by Dan H. McLachlan)*   zone   5

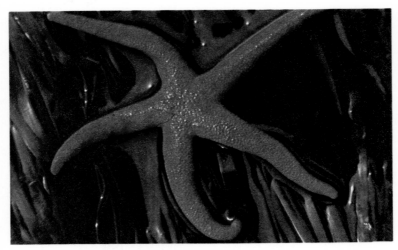

blood star, *Henricia leviuscula*   This smooth-surfaced star is brilliant orange-red on the dorsal side and light yellow below. It usually has five rays which are long and tapering. The madreporite filter is inconspicuous. The blood star is a filter feeder; the grooves on its ventral side have cilia which move the plankton-laden water to the mouth. *(Photo by Jak Ayres)*   zone 4

sun star, *Solaster stimpsoni*   This broad-disced star has eight to ten slender rays, is eight to fifteen inches (20-37 cm) across, and has a distinctive stripe of blue-gray that extends lengthwise to the tip of each ray, bordered by pink, red, or orange. Short, blunt spines evenly line the aboral surface. The sun star is usually seen in rocky areas below the tide line in the San Juan Islands, straits, and open coast. *(Photo by Dan H. McLachlan)* zones 4 , 5

rose star, *Crossaster papposus*   The concentric bands of red rose color make this star conspicuous. A network of tall calcareous stalks bristle on its dorsal surface. It has a broad disc with eight to fourteen rays and is about ten inches (25 cm) across. It is seldom exposed at low tide, and has been observed by the authors attacking and enveloping sea pens and weak sea stars with its strong arms. *(Photo by Dan H. McLachlan)*   zone   5

leather star, *Dermasterias imbricata*   A person can easily identify this star by its thick, soft, textured epidermis. Five short rays radiate from a broad disc. A light-colored madreporite filter is located near the center, and a leaden, blue-green to reddish color marks its dorsal side. Zipperlike grooves are evident on its ventral side. The leather star grows up to ten inches (25 cm) in diameter. It is often seen preying upon sea anemones in tide pools. *(Photo by Michael A. Kyte)*   zone   5

vermilion star, *Mediaster aequalis*   The vermilion star is fairly common at depths greater than fifty feet. A true star shape, it has a broad disc and tapering arms. It is six inches or less (15 cm) in diameter. The dorsal side has uniform calcareous plates resembling a mosaic. It eats sea pens, ascidians, algae, and sponges. *(Photo by Dan H. McLachlan)* zone   5

morning sun star, *Solaster dawsoni*   This star is present wherever there are significant numbers of sun stars, its primary food. Basic population dynamics can be observed in this predator - prey relationship. The larger morning sun star is similar in shape to its close relative and prey, the sun star, except that it is uniform in color, being usually orange, brown, or yellow. It commonly has eleven or thirteen rays and may be ten to eighteen inches (25-45 cm) across. *(Photo by Ronald L. Shimek)*   zones   4 , 5

ECHINODERMATA: class Echinoidea

If a person were to take a ten-legged sea star, exchange the tube feet on every other leg for spines made of calcite crystal, and then pin the points of all ten legs together over the top of the star, essentially what one would have would be a sea urchin or sand dollar of the class Echinoidea.

The round, calcareous skeletons of sea urchins and sand dollars are commonly sighted along Pacific Northwest beaches. Upon close examination, one finds that their skeletons have rows of tiny holes in them. In sand dollars these holes form a star-shaped pattern on the top. It is from these holes that the hydraulically-operated tube feet extend. Also, there are five broad bands of knobs radiating over the top surface of the sea urchin skeletons. Over these knobs the attaching sockets of the spines move to and fro by muscle action.

There is a second type of projection on urchins, scattered random-ly over their entire surface, called pedicellariae. They consist of a flexi-ble stalk with a knob at the end that is made up of three plierlike jaws. Pedicellariae have the specialized task of keeping all the other spines free of entangling debris and the waste excreted by the urchin from the center of its top (sand dollars have their anuses more conveniently located at their outer edges).

There is still a third type of projection on the surface of sea urchins called spaeridia. They happen to be the same sort of olfactory and tactile sensory tube feet that sea stars use to smell and touch with.

Sea urchins and sand dollars travel stilt fashion on the tips of their spines, which are intended as much for self-defense as locomotion, and they use their tube feet in conjunction to hold them in place to resist wave and current action and also to scale the faces of things. This is accomplished very nicely by the varieties of urchins that live in the Pacific Northwest, but in other parts of the world, where the size and shape of the spines are more like paddles or stubby fingers, movement is more difficult. Fortunately, urchins need not travel a great deal in their lifetimes.

The mouth of the urchin and sand dollar is at the center of the bottom, ventral side. It is large and has five teeth that encircle it from a tough kind of jaw that is called an Aristotle's lantern in honor of Aristotle who compared its shape to a type of lantern that existed in his time. Their gills also protrude from flaps around the mouth's opening. Urchins feed on seaweeds, kelps, dead animal matter, small organisms such as diatoms and microscopic plants, and even ingest sand for the microorganisms it contains.

Urchins and sand dollars are dioecious (of individual sexes) and have as many as five large gonads located under the tops of their shells. These gonads are connected to the center of the top by five ducts through which they discharge eggs or sperm. The eggs are fertilized in the water at random and quickly develop into free-swimming larvae called pluteus. These in turn metamorphose (change) in a complex way into carbon copies of their parents.

The same kind of eye spots that exist at the tips of sea star arms also exist with urchins and sand dollars. There are five of these photo-sensitive cells located around the center of their tops, but it is doubtful that they provide the organism with much useful information. Also located on the top is an opening leading to the same kind of madreporite filter that sea stars have and which provides the water needed to operate the tube feet.

Urchins live in all the Pacific Northwest ocean waters. On the coast, the purple urchins gain shelter from the heavy surf by carving caves out of the sandstone with their teeth and spines. Usually, however, urchins are out in the open, especially in the sheltered inland waters, slowly moving about in search of food. Sand dollars are usually more than half buried in the sand looking for microorganisms, and in some places they are so populous that they have shoved each other up on edge until they look like packages of cookies.

Urchins are eaten by fishes, sea stars, sea otters, men, and sea gulls (which break them open by flying up and dropping them onto the rocks). Early sailors would grind up sand dollars to make a purplish-black ink. It is important when examining sand dollars to replace them right side up because they are incapable of righting themselves and will perish on their backs. In examining urchins, one must be careful not to be accidentally impaled on their spines. The spines of urchins are very brittle and usually crumble under a person's flesh, causing infection. It may take many long months for the spines to finally be absorbed or rejected by the human body.

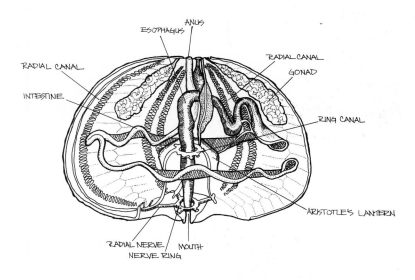

ANATOMY OF A SEA URCHIN

green sea urchin, *Strongylocentrotus droebachiensis*   Common, but with an uncommonly long scientific name, this urchin feeds largely on algae with its five sharp teeth (Aristotle's lantern). Its spines are small, short and crowded, while the test reaches about three inches (8 cm) in diameter. Green sea urchins are readily eaten by sea gulls when exposed or crowded into rock crevices at low tides. *(Photo by Judy Wagner)*   zones 4 , 5

giant red sea urchin, *Strongylocentrotus franciscanus*   The giant red sea urchin has long spines three inches (8 cm) in length, and a test up to six inches (15 cm) in diameter. It may live in huge colonies, inhabiting crevices in rocks from Alaska to Mexico. A food competitor of the abalone, it feeds on algae as well as small barnacles. *(Photo by Dan H. McLachlan)*   zones 4 , 5

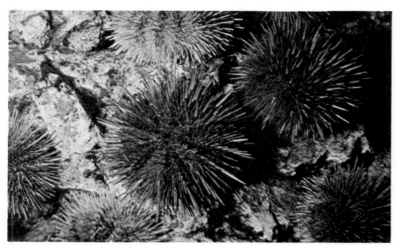

purple sea urchin, *Strongylocentrotus purpuratus* Pictured here among green sea urchins, the purple sea urchin may reach three inches (7.5 cm) in diameter. Its stubby spines are about an inch (2.5 cm) long and do not stand straight up as in other species. This urchin prefers coastal waters where there is plenty of wave action. *(Photo by Ronald L. Shimek)* zones 4 , 5

sand dollar, *Dendraster excentricus* This dark purple-brown creature has a soft, velvety covering consisting of short spines and tube feet. The sand dollar feeds on diatoms, other plankton, and sand grains covered with algae. It has a jaw system like other urchins, though modified for eating smaller material. *Dendraster* is unable to right itself and will die if turned over, which explains why many are seen on the seashore after storms. *(Photo by Jak Ayres)* zones 4 , 5

ECHINODERMATA: class Holothuroidea

Unlike other echinoderms, sea cucumbers and gherkins (holo-thuroids) have long leathery bodies. The protective armor of these animals is reduced to mere microscopic limy plates, called ossicles, that are just under the skin. Also, the axis of symmetry runs from the mouth to the anus. They lie sluggishly on the bottom like large, wart-covered worms, or burrow into the sand or mud so that only a small portion of their bodies is exposed. They exist in shallow waters and in deep waters as well, and occasionally they can be found on the sides of pilings and on the submerged timbers of docks.

The tube feet that are so prevalent with sea stars and urchins are also used by sea cucumbers for locomotion; only the madreporite filter of cucumbers is inside its water-filled body, rather than exposed to the outside. Certain species also have tube feet on their backs to assist them in burrowing and to provide tactile senses. Others, such as the creeping pedal cucumber (*Psolus chitonoides*), have all their tube feet on their sides for locomotion.

The body walls of cucumbers have two sets of muscles. One set encircles the entire body and provides it with rigidity. The cucumber pumps itself tightly full of water, and these muscles place additional pressure on the water so that the cucumber becomes as firm as a thick-walled balloon. Fortunately, the sea cucumber is also capable of re-generating its internal organs. When they are attacked, they may pop near the anus when extreme pressure is applied so that their intestines rupture out (called enviseration).

The second set of muscles consists of five pairs of powerful, rubber-bandlike muscles that run the length of sea cucumbers along the insides of their body walls. These muscles can contract in such a way as to permit them to move in a wormlike fashion.

The mouths of cucumbers do not have cilia to bring in the food. Instead, they have from five to thirty retractable tentacles which look like colorful ferns.   These tentacles are coated with a sticky mucus that collects organic debris and plankton. Whenever a particular tentacle has accumulated enough nutrients in its branches, a cucumber will insert it into its mouth to lick them clean. This is a curious procedure to watch. It only takes a cucumber a few moments to lick a single tentacle, and then it is withdrawn and another is inserted in its place. These tentacles also have the dual functions of providing taste and smell senses, and in some species there are small statocysts at their bases. The nervous system radiates from a ring around the mouth to other parts of the body.

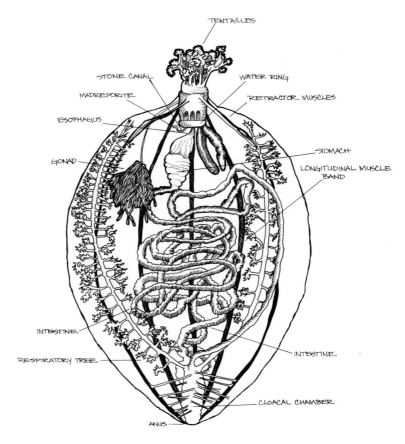

ANATOMY OF A HOLOTHUROID

The internal workings of sea cucumbers are also interesting. Their digestive tracts look like tangles of twine that end at the anus, and a pair of treelike respiratory organs that branch out from an enlargement of the rectum called the cloacal chamber. Remarkably enough, these respiratory trees act nearly like lungs and rhythmically pull in and expel water so that an exchange of gases can occur between the water and the blood in their walls.

One unusual means of self-defense some cucumbers have is a cluster of white, very sticky tubes, called cuvierian organs. When attacked, they are able to cast these out from their anus to confuse, entangle, and possibly poison their attacker. Certain small cucumbers are also able to break themselves into two parts, offering one part, it seems, to the predator while the remaining part continues to survive. Also, as has already been mentioned, cucumbers may pop if much pressure is applied to them, and their intestines, which are forced out into the water, distract the predator from the main organism.

Like sea stars and sea urchins, cucumbers are of separate sexes. However, besides releasing sperm or eggs into the water at random to develop into larvae called auricularia, several species also have brood pouches off to the sides of their mouths. Others raise their tiny offspring under their bodies to provide protection from predators until they reach greater maturity.

white sea gherkin, *Eupentacta quinquesemita*   The white sea gherkin has a bristly appearance because of its dark tube feet. Its length varies up to about three inches (7 cm). Though interesting to watch feeding on plankton, if handled, this sensitive animal expels its internal organs. Fortunately, it can regenerate them. This escape response is common to most sea cucumbers. *(Photo by Dan H. McLachlan)*   zone   5

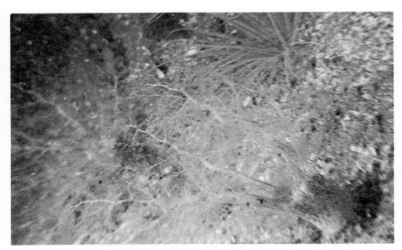

burrowing sea cucumber, *Leptosynapta clarki*   This tiny cucumber does not look much like a typical sea cucumber because it has microscopic calcareous anchors instead of tube feet covering its semitransparent skin. It varies in size, but a large specimen can be two to three inches (6-7 cm) long. Pinnately-branched tentacles encircle the mouth to process organisms attached to sand or other detritus. *(Photo by Dan H. McLachlan)*   zone   4

creeping pedal cucumber, *Psolus chitonoides*   The creeping pedal cucumber, abundant in deep water in Puget Sound, is about two inches (5 cm) in length and one inch (2.5 cm) wide. Its upper surface is brick red and covered with irregular calcareous plates. The ventral side is modified to adhere to subtidal rocks. A cylindrical neck bears beautiful branches of crimson tentacles which may be nearly as long as the body. *(Photo by Ronald L. Shimek)*   zones   4 , 5

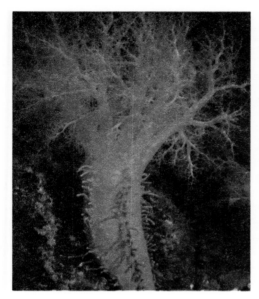

red sea gherkin, *Cucumaria miniata* The dark orange crown and ten clusters of branched tentacles are generally all that is visible of this animal, which exists in crevices and under rocks. The red sea gherkin moves sluggishly on tube feet that are situated lengthwise along five radii. This creature can change its shape and adhere to almost any nook. The body, four to eight inches (10-20 cm) long, resembles a fat worm when the tentacles are contracted. *(Photo by Ronald L. Shimek)* zones 4 , 5

red sea cucumber, *Parastichopus californicus* The red to brown surface of this creature is studded with soft, conical projections. It can reach seventeen inches (43 cm) in length and over three inches (8 cm) in diameter. Many tube feet are located on the semiflattened ventral side. The red sea cucumber extracts organic material from the sand and mud with its rootlike oral tentacles. *(Photo by Dan H. McLachlan)* zone 5

10.

MOLLUSCA: the Molluscs

The phylum Mollusca is a very large grouping of over one hundred thousand different species, and at one time it was even larger because it mistakenly included the Brachiopods and several Arthropods. Now the phylum has been narrowed down to include five classes of animals, Amphineura (the chitons), Gastropoda (snails, slugs, and nudibranchs), Bivalvia (clams and oysters), Scaphopoda (tusk shells), and Cephalopoda (squids and octopuses).

Most molluscs are marine inhabitants. They are free-living and are attached to rocks and wood; some are found burrowed into the sand and mud; some float; some crawl; and a few can swim. They have many things in common. Though not all share the characteristic of having limy shells, those that *do* have left a clear track through the pages of time which has been of great help to scientists. Mollusc shells deteriorate very slowly and are therefore ideal for becoming preserved in sandstone beds, thereby providing fossil information for researchers about evolution and the ages of different strata of rock.

Limy shelled molluscs have a thickened layer of flesh, called a mantle, which excretes layers of calcium carbonate to form the protective shells. Not all molluscs' mantles do this however (such as some nudibranchs and octopuses), and others may form more than one shell. Clams, for instance, have two shells that are called bivalves, and chitons have eight overlapping plates that look like shingles, called multivalves.

Molluscs have other features in common. For one, they have a muscular foot that can act like an undulating suction cup that propels them along or serves as a digging device to help them burrow into the sand. Most have a rasplike tongue covered with chitinous teeth, called a radula, which they can use for gathering food; a large digestive gland or liver; salivary glands to hasten digestion; a chambered heart; a kidney, called nephridium; and developed senses of touch, smell, taste, sight, and equilibrium. But what is most intriguing is that molluscs that live out of the water, such as the common lawn snail and banana slug, have developed pulmonary sacs or lungs just under their mantles, in which an exchange of gases can occur between the air and the blood in the walls of the sacs.

Molluscs eat almost anything, from decaying meat to plankton and algae.   Their diets may also alter as they mature.   Most are of different sexes; however, many are hermaphroditic and lay eggs either individually, in long strings, in leathery collars, or in beautiful, lacy, ribbonlike patterns.   A few are ovoviviparous—keep their eggs within themselves until they have developed into larvae.

Though a few molluscs live for only one year, many species live at least twenty-five years.   Some abalones may live for fifty years. What this means is that whenever an abalone is taken and eaten, it takes perhaps many long decades for another like it to take its place.   It is not surprising, in light of this fact, that overzealous abalone gatherers have seriously threatened whole populations along our coastal and inland shores.

MOLLUSCA: class Amphineura

Amphineurans, or chitons, are not easy creatures for predators to capture. This is due in part to the fact that they have eight over-lapping plates of armor that cover nearly their entire bodies. But also, they have very low silhouettes and each is held down to the rocks they dwell on by a most efficient muscular foot. The suction created by one square inch of a chiton foot creates as much as seventy pounds of pressure which makes them almost impossible to budge. The Pacific Northwest can boast of having the largest chitons in the world. The gum boot chiton, *Cryptochiton*, can reach a length of more than eight inches (20 cm) and theoretically can exert a total force of perhaps a thousand pounds or more. Should a predator somehow work a chiton free of its grip, the job is not over because the chiton will then roll itself into a tight ball just like a pill bug.

The armor plates of many chitons have tiny holes in them. These holes are the terminal points of nerve ends, which act as eye spots and also refract light to a certain extent. The plates are set in a tough, leathery border, called the girdle, and in the case of *Cryptochiton* this girdle completely covers the plates. There is a groove, called the pallial groove, on the underside of the girdle between its edge and the foot. The gills are located in the shelter of the pallial groove, and they resemble a fringe on a skirt.

Chitons have a mouth, a salivary gland, a small head, and a region between the mouth and esophagus which houses the toothy radula. Their diet consists of diatoms, seaweeds, and algae which they scrape from the surfaces of rocks with their radula. Their intestines are six or seven times the length of their bodies and lie in loose loops in their body cavities. Two pairs of nerve cords extend from a ring around the esophagus backwards, one pair to the foot and the other pair to form a closed loop at the base of the body cavity. These cords in turn give off a large number of lateral interconnecting nerves.

Chitons, like other molluscs, have a stomach, kidney, heart, liv-er, and large gonad. They are of separate sexes and fertilization in most cases occurs in the mantle cavity. Sperm leave the male in the exhalant currents from its gonad and are carried by inhalant currents into the pallial grooves of the female. The fact that chitons live grouped rather closely together facilitates fertilization. The eggs are issued singly in enclosed, spiny envelopes or in strings to the open water, but in certain species they are retained in the pallial groove between the gills, or even in the body cavity during the pre-larvae development. There can be up to two hundred thousand eggs discharged by a single female; this helps ensure the survival of chitons, which are vulnerable during their early stages of development.

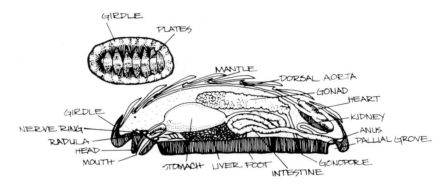

ANATOMY OF A CHITON

mossy chiton, *Mopalia muscosa*   Thought to be nocturnal, this tidal animal spawns in the late summer. The eight dorsal plates are surrounded by a narrow girdle that has many very stiff hairs or bristles. The mossy chiton is broadly ovate, with a body that averages around two and a half inches in length (6 cm). A mollusc, its ventral mouth harbors the rasplike tongue, called a radula, which it expends for scraping food from rocks. *(Photo by Jak Ayres)*   zones   3 , 4

lined chiton, *Tonicella lineata*   The beautiful lined chiton attains a length of about two inches (5 cm). It has dark brown lines wavering over backgrounds of yellows, oranges, pinks, and lavenders. A smooth, thin girdle encircles the margin. This chiton can be found grazing by day or night, usually amidst algae. *(Photo by Jak Ayres)*   zones   3 , 4

gum boot or giant chiton, *Cryptochiton stelleri*   Hard to identify as a chiton because its plates are covered by a thick, red-brown girdle, this animal ranges usually at night at the low tide mark and deeper. The gum boot can reach a length of more than eight inches (20 cm), making it the world's largest chiton. *(Photo by Jak Ayres)*   zones   4 , 5

black or leather chiton, *Katharina tunicata*   This chiton is distinguished by the black leathery girdle which covers all but about a third of each plate. The plates are mostly brown and may have limpets or barnacles adhering to them. Active both night and day, it may be three to six inches (8-15 cm) long. The foot is dull yellow-orange with a row of numerous separate gills along each side. *(Photo by Jak Ayres)*   zone   4

MOLLUSCA: class Gastropoda

Snails, slugs, whelks, nudibranchs, limpets, and abalones are all molluscs that share the same class, Gastropoda. There are over thirty-five thousand living species and another fifteen thousand fossil species of gastropods, which makes Gastropoda the largest class of Mollusca. They are an extremely well-distributed and adaptive class that can be found in oceans, in fresh water, and on the land.

Gastropods share many of the physical traits of chitons, but one characteristic that many species have that sets them apart is a radical twisting or coiling of not only their shells, but of their bodies, to form spirals. Another characteristic that sets them apart is the elongation of their ventral foot, and the ability on the part of many species to completely withdraw their soft bodies into their protective shells by means of the columella muscle which runs the length of their bodies and is connected to the shell at its apex.

Gastropods have large heads which have retractable tentacles protruding from them. Each of these tentacles has an eye at the end with a cornea, lens, and retina. Remarkably enough, in the case of certain pelagic (open-water) sea snails, these tiny eyes are more developed than even those of some fishes. The tentacles also contain smell and touch cells to provide additional sensory data for the animals.

Gastropods also have equilibrium organs called statocysts. These organs exist in animals as simple as jellyfishes, but those of gastropods are more developed. Basically all a statocyst is, is a vesicle or sac that has sensory cells with projecting bristles lining its walls. Attached to the tips of the bristles are one or more calcareous knobs (called statoliths), and when the animal is tilted, the gravitational pull on these knobs makes them tug against the sensory bristles. The animal may then respond and right itself. These equilibrium organs, along with the eyes, tentacles, radula, foot, gills and so forth, are all linked to one another through a system of somewhat complex, interconnected nerve clusters, or ganglia, which coordinate their functions.

The vascular systems of some of the gastropods consist of a two-chambered heart and, among land dwellers, pulmonary sacs or lungs situated in their mantle cavities where the blood is aerated in a network of blood vessels.   The rhythmic in-flow and out-flow of air occurs through a respiratory pore which is visible in slugs to the naked eye.

Among marine gastropods, respiration takes place with gills. Among some nudibranchs, however, gills have mostly disappeared and have been replaced by a secondary set of external branches, called cerata. Respiration occurs through the surface of these colorful cerata, and nudibranchs can be grouped by whether their cerata are club-shaped, leaf-shaped, and if they are clumped or are branched out in rows the length of the nudibranch's body. Whichever, they add coloration and decorativeness to these creatures and make them a pleasure to see and to photograph.

Reproduction among gastropods is considered rather advanced as, in most species, the males and females copulate by means of a penis and vagina. In some cases this copulation may be reciprocal with each animal containing both sets of sex organs. The gelatinous-covered eggs usually hatch into minute gastropods which are capable of sustaining life on their own.

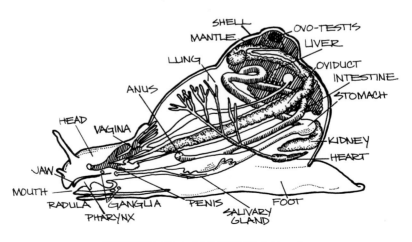

ANATOMY OF A GASTROPOD (SNAIL)

As any gardener knows, gastropods are hearty eaters. Though the majority of them are carnivorous, many marine species are omnivorous and relish both plant and animal life. With the help of their radulae, they will eat certain anemones and echinoderms, and will even bore into other molluscs and feed on them (the moon snail, *Polinices lewisii*, is an example). In turn, gastropods are eaten chiefly by fishes, birds, and mammals such as sea otters and people. For those that have shells, defense lies in pulling their soft bodies into their shells and, in many cases, sealing themselves in with a kind of thin door (operculum) that is especially designed for this as part of their foot. For the nudibranchs, which have no shells, defense is more of a problem. Some species, such as the sea lemon (*Archidoris montereyensis*), simply rely on secreting copious quantities of slime to ruin their predators' appetites. Others have developed the remarkable ability of passing the nematocysts of the anemones they are feeding on intact through their digestive systems and out to the tips of their cerata. These nematocysts, in turn, become their weapons for self-defense. Limpets and abalones, because of the shape of their shells, employ the same basic defense as chitons by simply hanging on tight in hopes that their predators cannot pull them loose.

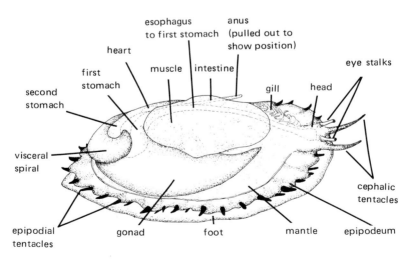

ANATOMY OF AN ABALONE

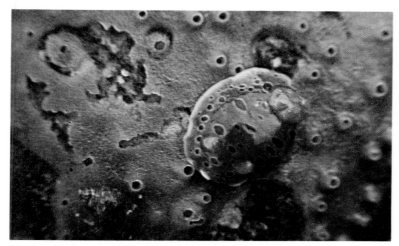

ringed nudibranch, *Diaulula sandiegensis*   The ringed nudibranch (shown here feeding on crumb-of-bread sponge) is easy to recognize because of its irregular dark rings, which are outlined in yellow or cream. This sea slug reaches about two and a half inches (6 cm) in length and an inch (2.5 cm) wide. It produces spirals of white egg ribbons most of the year. *(Photo by Jak Ayres)*   zones 3 , 4 , 5

sea lemon, *Archidoris montereyensis*   This plump-bodied, tidal nudibranch is yellow with patches of black pigment on and around the tubercles. There are two tentacles on the dorsal surface and a circle of whitish featherlike gills surround the anus. The sea lemon is about two inches (5 cm) long. It commonly grazes on sponges. Note the beautiful lacelike string of eggs of this mollusc. *(Photo by Dan H. McLachlan)*   zones 4 , 5

yellow margined nudibranch, *Cadlina luteomarginata*   Yellow margined nudibranchs are broad and flat, reaching about two inches (5 cm) in length. Wide mantle margins extend beyond the foot. The edge of the foot and tips of the tubercles are usually yellow. Nudibranchs are often seen copulating. *(Photo by Michael A. Kyte)*   zones 5

giant nudibranch, *Dendronotus rufus*   The giant nudibranch attains a length of just over ten inches (26 cm). It has six to nine branching pairs of cerata, streaked with dark red, which contrast the white or grayish body. This species grazes on floats and eelgrass, feeding on polyps. *(Photo by Dan H. McLachlan)*   zone 5

opalescent nudibranch, *Hermissenda crassicornis* The one- to two-inch (2.5-5 cm) opalescent nudibranch is distinctly marked with numerous cerata that are orange banded and tipped with white. It consumes hydroids, ascidians, other molluscs, eggs, and even pieces of fish. This type of nudibranch (eolid) is capable of storing the stinging cells of hydroids in its cerata. *(Photo by Dan H. McLachlan)* zone 5

striped nudibranch, *Armina californica* Lengthwise stripes of white, dark brown or black make it easy to recognize this species. The striped nudibranch may be seen plowing along in the sand searching for sea pens, which it preys upon. It grows up to three inches (8 cm) long and three-fourths of an inch (2 cm) wide. *(Photo by Dan H. McLachlan)* zone 5

alabaster nudibranch, *Dirona albolineata*   This translucent nudibranch may grow as large as three inches (7 cm). Remarkable leafy cerata are outlined with brilliant white lines. The alabaster nudibranch can crack small snail shells with its jaws. Besides snails, it consumes ascidians and bryozoans. *(Photo by Judy Wagner)*   zone   5

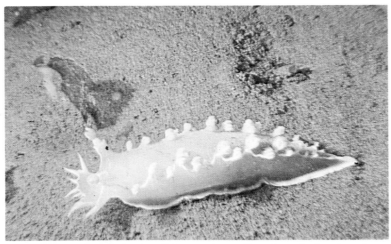

pink nudibranch, *Tritonia festiva*   This attractive nudibranch can be found grazing on sandy bottoms below the low tide line. The pink nudibranch is off-white or pink, with two rows of plumed gills which are usually lighter in color. It reaches a length of nearly five inches (12 cm). *(Photo by Dan H. McLachlan)*   zone   5

orange-spotted nudibranch, *Triopha carpenteri*   This stunning nudibranch, with orange-tipped papillae, tentacles, gills, and orange spots on a creamy body, can grow to a length of three inches (7 cm). In tide pool performances it may be seen upside down, suspended by threads of mucus. The orange-spotted nudibranch grazes on bryozoan colonies. Like most sea slugs, it gives off unpleasant secretions and therefore is not preyed upon. *(Photo by Judy Wagner)*   zone 5

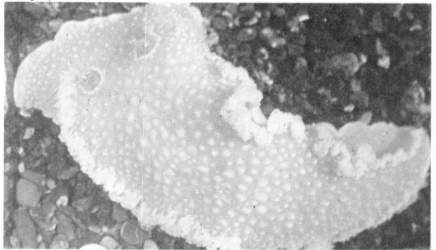

lemon peel nudibranch, *Tochuina tetraquetra*   Common to the San Juan Islands, this large Pacific Northwest nudibranch attains a length of twelve inches (30 cm). The body is yellow with two rows of plumed gills of lighter color along its sides. *Tochuina* lives about three years, and preys upon sea pens and sea whips. *(Photo by Ken Conte)*   zone 5

leafy horn-mouth, *Ceratostoma foliatum   Ceratostoma* has three broad winglike projections which run longitudinally along its shell. The coloration will vary, and it may reach three inches (8 cm) in length. The fanglike tooth on its outer lip may be used to hook the ridges of barnacles while feeding on them. This snail also preys upon many bivalves. Its eggs, which it deposits on its own shell or on rocks, are bright yellow, and the cases are stalked. *(Photo by Jak Ayres)*   zone   4

wrinkled purple snail, *Thais lamellosa*   The shape and color of this snail's shell seem to depend on the wave action, current, and its diet. Usually the shell has seven whorls and ridges, which may be elevated and wrinkled at the edges. The wrinkled purple snail lays stalked, translucent yellow, rice-sized egg cases that hang in large clusters under rocks and ledges. It feeds primarily on barnacles. *(Photo by Jak Ayres)*   zone   4

dogwinkle, *Thais emarginata*   The dogwinkle snail is common on rocky shores. It is about an inch (2.4 cm) long. The shell has five whorls and heavy ribs spaced with delicate ones. The color of the shell varies, but the ribs are usually white with patterns of yellows, browns, or black in the grooves. The opening is over half the height of the shell. *(Photo by Jak Ayres)*   zones 2 , 3 , 4

Oregon or hairy triton, *Fusitriton oregonensis*   A large snail reaching four inches (10 cm) in length, the Oregon triton is a voracious predator. It attacks sea urchins and most bivalves, drilling holes in their shells and devouring the soft inner bodies. This species has a conspicuous brown bristly epidermis (periostracum) growing on its shell, which hydroids, tube worms, and barnacles attach themselves to. *(Photo by Ken Conte)*   zone 5

Sitka periwinkle, *Littorina sitkana*   This is one of many periwinkles found grazing high in intertidal areas. It has spiral grooves which form continuous ridges on its three whorls. The fat shell of the Sitka periwinkle may be a half an inch (1.5 cm), and ranges in color from grays to red. Completely adapted to the intertidal life, these snails would die if not allowed air. *(Photo by Jak Ayres)*   zones 2 , 3

hooked slipper shell, *Crepidula adunca*   Slipper shells have a horizontal plate which forms a well developed white shelf on the inside of the shell. The hooked slipper shell has a hook-shaped peak on its posterior slope that, upon first glance, is often thought to be a limpet. It is usually brown, and may be seen hitching rides on turban snails and limpets. *(Photo by Thomas H. Suchanek)*   zones 4 , 5

blue top shell, *Calliostoma ligatum*   The seven whorls of this species are spirally sculp-
tured with contrasting ridges of light and dark browns. Its maximum height is about an
inch (2.5 cm). This snail is seen intertidally and deeper, grazing on diatoms and other
algae. The common name indicates the "top" shape, and when the outer layer of shell has
become worn, it shows the bluish pearl layer. *(Photo by Bob Turner)*   zone   4

ringed top shell, *Calliostoma annulatum*   To fully appreciate the beauty of this snail, it
must be seen alive among the kelps and eelgrass. It is about an inch high (2.5 cm) and has
eight or nine whorls. The whorls are somewhat flattened, with colored beading and
symmetrical purple bands along the margins. The ringed top snail eats hydroids. *(Photo
by Ken Conte)*   zones   4 , 5

moon snail, *Polinices lewisii*   The beautiful, white moon snail is sometimes as much as five inches (13 cm) in diameter. The large body aperature is closed by a thick operculum when the animal withdraws into its protective shell; but when it is out looking for bivalves to devour, its mantle covers the shell profusely. During spring and summer, eggs are laid in interesting collarlike shapes, as shown below. *(Photo by Dan H. McLachlan)*   zones 3 , 4 , 5

sand collar - moon snail egg case   The eggs of the moon snail are sandwiched between a mucus and sand mixture. The width of the egg case is the same size as the opening of the snail's shell. *(Photo by Jak Ayres)*   zones 3 , 4 , 5

black turban, *Tegula funebralis*   The black turban is similar to other turban snails, except that this species has a rounded light-colored apex. The main shell color is blackish-purple, and there are usually about four wrinkled body whorls. It grazes on algae and seaweeds. *(Photo by Kenneth P. Sebens)*   zones 3 , 4

dire or spindle whelk, *Searlesia dira*   This whelk is common on rocky shores in the intertidal zone, where it grows to over an inch (3 cm) in length. The general coloring is gray,
and it has numerous fine spiral ridges. A carnivore, it feeds on barnacles, worms, and
injured animals. *(Photo by Jak Ayres)*   zone 4

flat abalone, *Haliotis walallensis*   As its name implies, the flat abalone has a low profile.
Its shell reaches a length of over five inches (13.5 cm). The shell is usually green and/or
red with stripes and bands on the outside, and pearly white on the inside. Unlike the pinto
abalone which is found intertidally, the flat abalone is seldom seen shallower than eighty
feet. *(Photo by Peter C. Howorth)*   zone 5

pinto abalone, *Haliotis kamtschatkana*   This animal is found intertidally, and deeper, grazing on the algae covering rocks. The shell, often encrusted, reaches five inches (10-13 cm) or more in length and is straight with a wavy surface. The epipodeum of the pinto is light yellow with brown splotches and sometimes orange fringes, whereas the epipodeum of the flat abalone is off-white splotched with brown and yellow. *(Photo by Jak Ayres; courtesy of the Seattle Aquarium)*   zones 4 , 5

whitecap limpet, *Acmaea mitra*   This thick, conical limpet is usually about one inch (2.5 cm). The white shell is commonly seen overgrown with the encrusting coralline red alga *(Lithothamnion)* it grazes upon. The whitecap limpet has a powerful foot that holds it to the rocks of its current-swept habitat. *(Photo by Jak Ayres)*   zone 4

finger limpet, *Collisella digitalis*   This deeply-ribbed limpet has an apex projecting forward from the edge of its shell. The colors alternate with the ribs from browns to grays. The finger limpet may be found high in the intertidal zone, often in the moist cracks in rocks feeding on algae. Most adults are an inch (2.5 cm) in diameter. *(Photo by Jak Ayres)*   zones 2 , 3

plate limpet, *Notoacmea scutum*   The plate limpet has a flat, smooth shell marked with concentric, radiating lines and an apex near the middle. About one and a half inches (4 cm) long, it may be seen grazing on diatoms low in the intertidal zone. *(Photo by Jak Ayres)*   zones 3 , 4

keyhole limpet, *Diodora aspera*   The characteristic hole on the apex of this species allows water to flow from the body. The shell has radiating ridges crossed by minute concentric lines. This two-inch (5 cm) animal often has a scale worm living between the foot and mantle. The reason for this interesting relationship is not known. When approached by the leather sea star, the keyhole limpet will extrude its fleshy mantle up over the shell, making it very difficult for the sea star to grasp it. *(Photo by Jak Ayres)*   zone 4

shield limpet, *Collisella pelta*   This confusing limpet may be ribbed and have a wavy margin, or have no ribs at all and have a smooth margin. The apex of the shield limpet is well back of the anterior edge. It may be one and a half inches (4 cm) long, and may be seen grazing on rocks exposed at low tide. *(Photo by Thomas H. Suchanek)*   zone 2 , 3

MOLLUSCA: class Bivalvia

Among animal populations, there are numbers living on the fringes that may slowly adapt and specialize in order to survive away from the others under differing conditions. Bivalves are an example of this adaptation, for on the whole they have become specialized to live away from the hard surfaces preferred by most other molluscs. They have instead taken up residences in the soft, sandy or muddy bottoms, or in some cases have bored into wood or soft stone or even tied themselves to vertical surfaces like so many alpine rock climbers. One species has gone so far as to clip itself onto the undersides of sea stars in a commensal relationship.

The class Bivalvia is comprised of clams, mussels, oysters, scallops, pectens, and geoducks, among others. They live in both fresh water and salt water, and though certain species have been found as deep as thirty-seven thousand feet, generally they prefer the shallows. Enclosed in rigid shells of two parts, they are known as bivalves. Their shells provide their soft bodies with support, and in most cases they can tightly close themselves in for protection from predators and the elements.

The shells of bivalves are made up of three layers. The outer layer, called the periostracum, is thin, colored, and provides protection against corrosive elements in the water. A thick middle layer, called the perismatic layer, is a hard configuration of crystalline calcium carbonate. Both of these outer layers are formed by the outer edges of the bivalve's mantle, and their growth is marked in ridges—the broader ones can be counted like the rings in a tree to determine the animal's age in years. Finally, the inner layer, the nacre, or mother-of-pearl, is a build-up of many fine layers of beautiful, iridescent calcium carbonate which the entire mantle membrane produces in order to add additional thickness to the growing shells.

At the point where the two shells of bivalves join, there are several, rounded, toothlike projections on the shell edges. These act as guides and pivot points so that the shells will be properly aligned when they close. Between the hinge teeth is a very tough, hard, flexible hinge ligament which strengthens the juncture. Also involved are one or two strong muscles, called adductors, that are attached to the inner surfaces of the two valves (shells) and pull them shut with tremendous force. In the case of some bivalves, such as geoducks, the body is too large to allow complete closure.

What most people mistakenly call the "neck" of these creatures is not a neck at all, but pairs of tubes or siphons. On the surfaces of the large mantle cavity are cilia which pull water in through the larger incurrent siphon and push used water out the smaller excurrent siphon. Bivalves are filter feeders, and so, besides providing the gills with oxygenated water, these siphons also draw in a diet of plankton.

An adaptation of the gills is the secret of bivalves' success. As with other molluscs, bivalves have a pair of gills; however, they have gone a step further and have folded their gills over to form two pairs of gills that look and act very much like car radiators. These folded gills are covered with mucus and cilia which enable them not only to carry out respiration, but to entrap plankton in the mucus layers and to move it by means of the cilia to their bottom edges and from there down a groove to the fleshy, liplike labial palps that surround the mouth, and then to the mouth itself.

Though they are a bit more sophisticated, the digestive tracts of bivalves are basically like most molluscs, but being filter feeders, they have no radulae. They have a mouth, esophagus, stomach, intestine, anus, liver, two kidneys, a kidney aperture, and an enzyme-producing organ to help break down starches. The heart pumps oxygenated blood and dissolved nutrients to all parts of the body, disposes of carbon dioxide in the gills and mantle, and rids the animal of organic wastes through the kidneys. Their reduced nervous system is also quite similar to the other molluscs, only they have photosensitive cells in the margins of their siphons, and touch cells in the edges of the mantle and in the foot. In addition they have an organ called an osphradium, which is located in the incurrent siphon, that tests the incoming water for silt content. If the intake of silt exceeds the capacity of the bivalve, the osphradium triggers a reduction in water intake.

Bivalves are dioecious. Their gonads are quite large and expel sperm and eggs in huge quantities (through ducts located near their kidney apertures) directly into open water. Since fertilization occurs by chance, the quantities involved here must be great. A single female oyster, for instance, may put out as many as sixty million eggs in a single season. The eggs hatch into spat ciliated larvae that eventually drop to the bottom where they crawl about for a time before attaching or burrowing and maturing into adults.

Bivalves have been very successful at surviving where most other molluscs could not, and up until the advent of Man, their greatest enemy was only certain types of sea stars. However, like the sponges and corals, they depend on the plankton in the water for their nutrition, and consequently, they are among the first to suffer from pollutants. When clam and oyster beds begin to grow sick and die as they have in so many parts of the world, it's time for men to determine the causes and to take immediate steps to correct the situation.

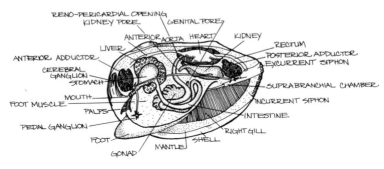

ANATOMY OF A BIVALVE

Olympia or native oyster, *Ostrea lurida*   The population of this west coast oyster has rapidly declined in recent years because of pollutants, freshwater dilutions, silt run-off from construction, overharvesting, and temperature fluctuations. The grayish shell is not more than two inches in diameter (5 cm), with the valves nearly equal in size. Olympia oysters may change sex from one season to the next. *(Photo by Jak Ayres)*   zone   4

Japanese or Pacific oyster, *Crassostrea gigas*   The fluting on the external surface of the Japanese oyster's shell is always prominent. This common oyster comes in separate sexes and may exceed a foot in length (30 cm). Snails, sea stars, boring sponges, worms, crabs, skates, and people prey upon them. *(Photo by Jak Ayres)*   zone   4

Pacific pink scallop, *Chlamys hastata*   This scallop is about two inches long and one and a half inches wide (5 by 4 cm). It has twenty-four fanlike spiny ribs radiating on a rose-pink shell. Normally it will lie with the right valve against the bottom. The Pacific pink scallop can attach itself to the substrate with threads (byssus) or swim freely by a sort of jet propulsion, clapping the valves together and forcing the water out through an opening near the hinge. *(Photo by Ronald L. Shimek)*   zone   5

smooth pecten, *Chlamys rubida*   The right valve of this species is whitish with close-set, almost smooth ribs. The left valve is rose pink. Like the Pacific pink scallop, the upper valve is commonly encrusted with a sponge. Both these species are about the same size. They occur in beds below the low tide mark. *(Photo by Bob Turner)*   zone   5

purple-hinged rock scallop, *Hinnites giganteus*   The purple-hinged rock scallop is free-swimming when young but settles when about an inch long (2.5 cm), attaching the right valve of its shell permanently to rocks. The upper shell becomes encrusted with barnacles, hydroids, tube worms, and boring sponges. Its diameter may exceed six inches (15 cm). Sexes can be determined by looking between the valves of a feeding animal. Males have white gonads, females' gonads are red. *(Photo by Jak Ayres)*   zone 5

rock oyster or jingle shell, *Pododesmus macroschisma*   This oyster can modify its shape to fit place of attachment; however, the thin valves are usually round and grow to five inches (13 cm) in diameter. The lower shell has a notched hole through which the byssus extrudes to fasten the shell to rock. *(Photo by Dan H. McLachlan)*   zones 4 , 5

blue or edible mussel, *Mytilus edulis*   This small, blue-black (sometimes brownish) mussel is seldom more than two inches long (5 cm), somewhat wedge shaped, and thin-shelled. These bivalves are filter feeders that attach themselves to the substrate in clusters. They can move slowly by throwing byssus threads in the direction they wish to go. *(Photo by Jak Ayres)*   zone   3

California mussel, *Mytilus californianus*   Found more often on exposed coasts than in the sheltered waters of Puget Sound, this thick-shelled mussel may be ten inches (25 cm) in length. The shells are usually black, but may have white streaks on them. In the summer months the California mussel is known to absorb high quantities of toxin from filtering the waters of the organism responsible for "red tide" *(Gonyaulax)*. *(Photo by Jak Ayres)* zone   3

heart cockle, *Clinocardium nuttallii*   The heart cockle is two to four inches long (5-10 cm). Its thick shell has lines radiating from the umbo with deep grooves between them. Capable of amazing movement, the heart cockle uses its foot to flip away from a predator. It prefers the low tide line on mud and sandy beaches, and will be on or just below the surface. Yearly growth rings on the shell reveal the age and types of seasons this clam has endured. *(Photo by Jak Ayres)*   zone   4

butter clam, *Saxidomus giganteus*   The butter clam has a thick, white or off-white shell marked by concentric growth lines. It is usually about three inches (8 cm) long and lives in gravel beaches down as deep as fourteen inches (20-35 cm). It frequently houses commensal crabs in its mantle cavity, and may live longer than twenty years. *(Photo by Jak Ayres)*   zones   3 , 4

littleneck clam, *Protothaca staminea*   Also called a "steamer," this clam is common in the Pacific Northwest. The shell is fairly thick and up to two and a half inches (6 cm) in length. Valves may be marked with earthy colors, often in interesting designs. The littleneck lives near the surface of mixed gravel-sand beaches. Using a shovel to dig these and other clams will often kill more than two for every one captured; a forked spade is suggested by most experts. *(Photo by Jak Ayres)*   zones 3 , 4

bent-nosed clam, *Macoma nasuta*   The bent-nosed clam is so-named because the posterior end of the shell turns upward. It is about two inches long (5 cm) at most and lives four to six inches down (10-15 cm) in mostly muddy beaches. It will extend an incurrent siphon above the mud when feeding. This species is capable of living in muddy, polluted, and brackish waters. Its presence may indicate low oxygen concentrations in the water. *(Photo by Jak Ayres)*   zones 3 , 4 , 5

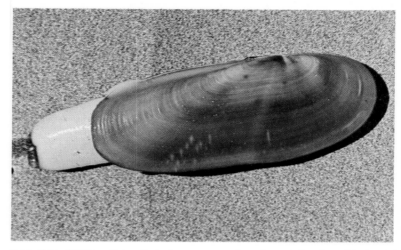

razor clam, *Siliqua patula* Preferring open coasts and sandy beaches, this hunted species is a fast digger and can travel a foot (30 cm) in seven seconds. The shells are fragile and are up to six inches (15 cm) long and two and a half inches (6.5 cm) wide. The outer shells have a brown or yellowish-brown varnished appearance, while inside they are pearly white. *(Photo by Jak Ayres)* zone 4

horse or gaper clam, *Tresus capax* One of the largest clams, the horse clam can be identified by a round "squirt hole" in the neck, out of which water may shoot two or three feet (30-60 cm). The shell is white with wrinkled pieces of brown or blue "skin" over the margin. The valves are uneven and may attain a length of eight inches (20 cm). When retracted, the siphon remains outside the shell. *(Photo by Jak Ayres)* zone 4

mud clam or soft-shell clam, *Mya arenaria*   Introduced to the Pacific Northwest some fifty years ago with seed oysters from the Atlantic coast, the mud clam grows up to six inches long (15 cm). The white or gray shells are fragile and have uneven concentric sculpture patterns. It thrives in mixtures of sand and mud near river mouths. *(Photo by Jak Ayres)*   zones   3 , 4

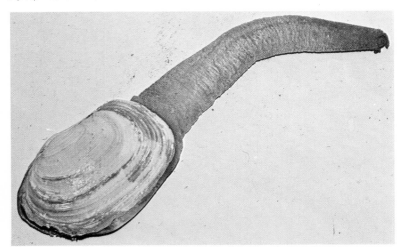

geoduck, *Panopea generosa*   These enormous clams may have eight-inch (20 cm) chalk-white shells. Their siphons may hang out an equal length when fully contracted, and up to three feet (.9 m) when relaxed. An average specimen weighs about six pounds (2.7 kg), but they can weigh three times that much. Geoducks generally live two or three feet (60-90 cm) deep in soft mud or loose sand. *(Photo by Jak Ayres)*   zones   4 , 5

rough piddock, *Zirfaea pilsbryi* This large clam uses the ridges on its valves like teeth to saw back and forth so it can bore into limestone, shale, or clay. Its burrowing power comes from the foot and adductor muscles. The four-inch (10 cm) shell is open at both ends so that the animal is incompletely covered. The rough piddock remains in its solid burrow for a lifetime. *(Photo by Dan H. McLachlan)* zones 3 , 4 , 5

shipworm, *Bankia setacea* The shipworm is a clam in a wormlike shape, Its anterior end has small shells which, when rocked back and forth, bore through wood. The burrows generally follow the grain of the wood and will rarely, if ever, penetrate another burrow. Although the wood passes through this mollusc's digestive tract, shipworms are primarily filter feeders. *(Photo by Jak Ayres)* zones 3 , 4 , 5

MOLLUSCA: class Cephalopoda

Special consideration should be given octopuses because they are such misunderstood personalities. And there is no denying it, out of water this giant cephalopod (a class shared by nautiluses and squids) looks like a pile of entrails from a gutted cow. They are also slimy to the touch, ice cold, and have a nasty tendency to glom onto curious fingers in a most determined, unsettling fashion. A well-known marine biologist once said that nothing in nature is more gruesome and hideous than the sinuous writhing of these creatures. Even John Steinbeck, in his book *Cannery Row* wrote of the octopus, "Then the creeping murderer, the octopus, steals out, slowly, softly, moving like a gray mist, pretending now to be a bit of weed, now a rock, now a lump of decaying meat while its evil goat eyes watch coldly...It leaps savagely on the crab, there is a puff of black fluid, and the struggling mass is obscured with the sepia cloud while the octopus murders the crab."

Admittedly, an octopus is not just another pretty face and has a bad reputation from being much maligned and misunderstood in the past. But in the water, the octopuses' natural habitat, this strange creature becomes a graceful ballerina, a sleight of hand artist, a prankster. He is shy and yet he is very curious and exploratory.

Three species of octopuses live in the Pacific Northwest. *Octopus leioderma* and *Octopus rubescens* are not commonly seen and are small, growing to a diameter of six to eight inches (15-20 cm). But the male members of the species *Octopus dofleini* are the largest of all octopuses in the world and are reputed to grow to a diameter of thirty feet (9.2 m). In Hood Canal, the authors have seen them measuring close to twenty feet (6.1 m) in diameter. However, seven-foot (2.1 m) males are the most common size.

Female *O. dofleini* do not grow over five or six feet (under 1.8 m) across due to the fact that they perish while raising their young. When the females are bred, a male octopus donates with one arm a pencil-shaped, transparent, gelatinous sack of sperm to her by simply inserting it deeply inside one of her large intake ports. She then searches about for a proper lair in which to lay her eggs. She seeks a cave twice her size which has an opening so small she can barely make it through, even after extruding her body down to an amazingly thin shape. As her last legs slither from sight, they attach themselves to one or more rocks. These she pulls in with her to block the cave entrance against the intrusion of rockfishes and hungry wolfeels.

Octopuses' eggs are the size and color of white rice and hang from the roof of the lair like thick clumps of grapes on black stems. There are approximately one or two quarts of these, and it is the female's job to look after them. Most sources agree that it takes from two to three months for these eggs to turn color and hatch as viable, miniature octopuses, but from our observations of Puget Sound's *dofleinis*, it can take as long as six months for the hatching process. During that time the mother uses nozzlelike funnels on the sides of her head to constantly wash water over and through the cluster of eggs to keep them clean and to constantly supply them with oxygenated water. To avoid contamination and to avoid the risk of leaving the lair unattended in order to hunt, she does not eat during these long months but lives on the fats and proteins of her own body tissue. The female will shrink to half her original size during the incubation period, and then, on the week when the eggs finally begin to hatch (much to the delight of rockfishes that wait outside the lair for the tiny, pulsing tidbits that try to make their escape to open water) she has so consumed herself that she dies within the cave, now no more than a pale heap of skin.

Octopuses are born with large pigmentation cells, called chromatophores, that can be contracted or expanded at will, to change color. The octopus can change from mottled white to deep red and brown faster than any living creature (one-tenth of a second), and when it combines this talent with its ability to ooze into tiny spaces and make its skin take on the texture of its surroundings with highly developed papillae on its skin, it has a certain amount of defense against being spotted and attacked by its three greatest predators, wolfeels, lingcods, and scuba divers. Its beak, deeply set in the white flesh at the apex of its arms, is a black horny nipper arrangement that resembles a parrot's beak. It only uses this to help it crack crab, however, and except for a small venomous Australian species, it is difficult to get one to use its beak in self-defense.

People are beginning to temper their hostile attitudes towards the octopus. This is accountable in part to the fact that this creature will often reach out and almost affectionately drape one of its arms over a diver who has settled down to watch it. Also, there is an almost human quality about an octopus's eye and eyebrow that is not seen with fishes, and often this makes people more sensitive to the creature's predicament. And, of course, once a person appreciates how clever the octopus can be at hunting and hiding, he often conveys this to other people who in turn temper their attitudes.

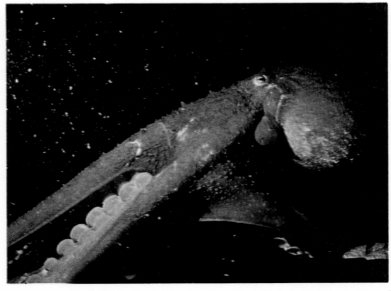

octopus, *Octopus dofleini*   Octopus in take-off position. *(Photo by Neil Hurd)*   zone 5

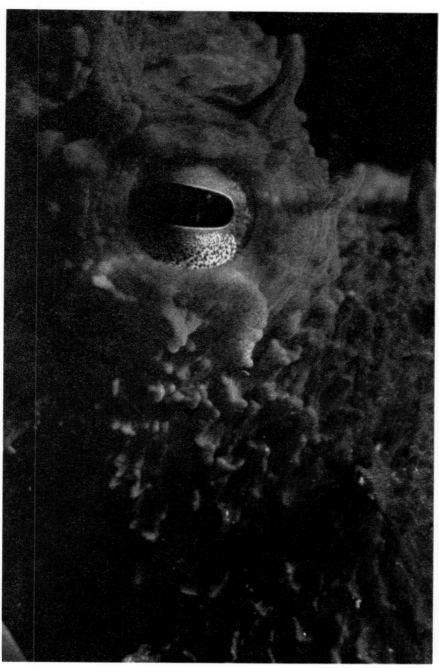

close up of an octopus' eye *(Photo by Dan H. McLachlan)*

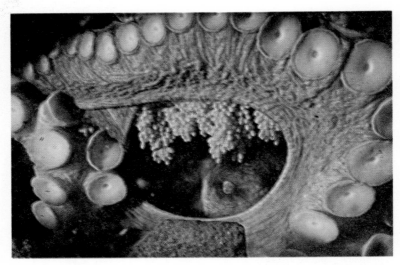

octopus, *Octopus dofleini*   Commonly found in Pacific Northwest waters, *O. dofleini* is the largest octopus in the world and may grow to a diameter of thirty feet (9 m). The female pictured here is protecting her rice-sized eggs which will hatch in six months. *(Photo by Don Bloye)*   zone   5

stubby squid, *Rossia pacifica*   The stubby squid is about five inches (12 cm) (size includes the thick unequal tentacles). It lives on muddy bottoms where it sometimes lies buried waiting for unsuspecting prey. A quick animal, it also uses its amazing ability to change color for defense and obtaining food. *(Photo by Ronald L. Shimek)*   zone   5

11.

ARTHROPODA: the   Crustaceans
subphylum: Chelicerata   classes: Pycnogonida, Arachnida
subphylum: Mandibulata   class: Crustacea

Arthropods perhaps arose from the segmented worms (annelids) to the point where in sheer numbers they dominate the earth. There are over seven hundred seventy-five thousand species of arthropods, which account for four-fifths of the known species of animals in the world, and many of these species have enormous populations.

Arthropods include crabs, shrimps, lobsters, and barnacles (which form the class Crustacea, the only class of arthropods dealt with in this book since they are the main marine animals of the phylum Arthropoda); the insects (Insecta, which account for a large portion of the immense population); the spiders, scorpions, and ticks (Arachnida); centipedes (Chilopoda); and millipedes (Diplopoda). Some zoologists arrange them in groupings other than these. What all these various classes of creatures share in common is a segmented exoskeleton that is jointed at various places to allow movement. This is also the first phylum in which a large percentage of its members have completely adapted to the land. They exist seemingly everywhere. And what is perhaps most significant about them is the fact that many of these species show an evolved social organization that involves division of labor and intra-colonial cooperation.

Like other arthropods, Crustacea have all their surfaces covered with a chitinous exoskeleton or cuticle. The cuticle is secreted by the epidermis (the outermost layer of skin) called the hypodermis. It can be smooth, rough, spiny, pitted, hard, or flexible. Among those species that have hard exoskeletons, the joint areas are covered only with a thin layer of cuticle so that the animal will be able to move. Even then, it is remarkable stuff which is made in various forms and for various purposes by all multicelled animals with the exception of the echinoderms and vertebrates. It is insoluable in water, alcohol, alkali, diluted acids, or the digestive juices of many animals. In short, it is an ideal material to provide armor protection against attack and the loss of body fluids. It is the one characteristic, above the others, that has permitted arthropods to be so successful at survival, not to mention their extreme strength.

On the other hand, one shortcoming of having their bodies covered by an exoskeleton is the fact that crustaceans and other arthropods must shed their hard coverings in order to grow. This happens from four to seven times in their lifetimes and is begun by the hypodermis secreting enzymes which dissolve the inside of the cuticle. When the hypodermis has freed itself, it secretes a new cuticle underneath, called the epicuticle, and then begins to molt the old. The epicuticle is impervious to the effects of the enzymes and is flexible enough to allow the arthropod to swell up with water to the point where it can break free of the deteriorated cuticle. Once free, it remains abnormally large until the combined actions of the water (or air) and chemical action harden the epicuticle to the new size. Once this has been accomplished, the animal has new growing room on the inside.

Arthropods' complex muscles, which are capable of extremely rapid action, are coordinated by a developed nervous system that also coordinates the functions of various specialized organs, such as antennae, sensory hairs, eyes, hearing organs, statocysts for equilibrium, claws, and jaws. They also have compound eyes at the ends of movable stalks. The compound eye is a complex, rounded arrangement of about two thousand five hundred tapered vision units each of which has a lens and the ability to form a part of a mosaic or opposition image that stimulates the nerve fibers linked to the optic nerve.

Crustaceans are solitary dwellers on the whole, and prefer to remain hidden in crevices, under rocks, and in abandoned snail shells. In fact, the population of hermit crabs is governed almost exclusively by the availability of empty shells. Some other species of crabs try to remain camouflaged by attaching debris to the tops of their exoskeletons, and have rough projections from their cuticles developed especially for this purpose. As a further means of self-defense, crustaceans are able to regenerate limbs that have been taken off by predators; in some cases they will actually give up limbs in hopes that predators will be satisfied and leave the rest of them alone. This phenomenon is called autotomy.

The diets of crustaceans consist of larvae, worms, small snails, fishes, dead animal matter, microorganisms, and other crustaceans. They are in turn eaten by certain fishes, octopuses, birds, and people, among others.

Except in the case of barnacles, the sexes are separate in crustaceans, and fertilization occurs within the females as a result of copulation. The eggs, which may number in the hundreds, develop in small cavities or follicles before being discharged from the females through openings located near two of the central walking legs. The larvae that hatch from these eggs may have several stages of development which happen to correspond to the animal's evolutionary history.

Barnacles, remarkably enough, are also crustaceans, despite the fact they look so unlike the others. They are unique among crustaceans in that they contain both sex organs and are enclosed, at least in part, in calcareous shells. Also, they are attached. In most cases barnacles prefer to be attached where there is a great deal of movement of the water. The reason for this is that they use delicately developed fanlike appendages to sweep microorganisms from the passing water into their mouths, and as a result they are found attached to rocks where there is active wave or current action. Some species attach themselves exclusively to the backs of crabs, turtles, or whales, and rely on their movements to bring nutrients within grasp.

goose-neck barnacle, *Pollicipes polymerus* This species of goose-neck barnacle can be found closely clustered on rocks in tidal areas along the Pacific Coast. The brownish stalk is approximately one half inch (1.8 cm) long and has a leathery texture. Eighteen or more white, calcareous plates protect the upper body, from which the cirri "net" plankton and minute crustaceans. Their colonies are usually set up facing the shore. This allows them to capture organisms in water running off rock outcroppings after waves break. *(Photo by Jak Ayres)* zones 2 , 3 , 4

goose-neck barnacle, *Lepas anatifera*   Normally attached to floating logs, bottles or kelps, this goose-neck barnacle is sometimes found washed up on shore. It often lives in large colonies. The "neck" of each animal is thin and light brown. Only four or five white plates make up the shell. *(Photo by Thomas H. Suchanek)*   zone 5

rock barnacle, *Balanus cariosus*   This barnacle lives near the low tide line and grows to a diameter of two inches (5 cm). Tall and cylindrical in tight groups, when scattered it will grow in the shape of a ridged cone. Two plates form the operculum that opens during feeding to allow the plumelike cirri to net plankton. Barnacles contain both male and female gonads and hold their eggs until they hatch into free-swimming larvae. *(Photo by Jak Ayres)*   zone 4

acorn barnacle, *Balanus glandula*   The acorn barnacle is the most abundant barnacle of the Pacific Northwest. It produces clouds of larvae that other plankton-eaters feed upon. A plankton-strainer itself, it is found encrusting rocks, pilings, boats and other available surfaces, including the backs of crabs. This barnacle reaches a diameter of half an inch (1.5 cm). The cone-shaped shell may form peaks. *(Photo by Jak Ayres)*   zones 2 , 3 , 4

giant barnacle, *Balanus nubilus*   This huge barnacle may be over three inches (8 cm) high, with a diameter at the base of five or six inches (15 cm). It lives in deep waters, usually in areas where currents remain steady. The appendages, which can easily be seen snaring plankton from the water, are actually legs which may rotate 90°. The stomach takes up most of its body. *(Photo by Dan H. McLachlan)* zones   4 , 5

green isopod, *Idotea wosnesenskii*   Of the four thousand or more species of isopods, this is one of the most common and easiest to recognize. It is seen among kelps, on floats, or in mussel beds. The green isopod may be one and a half inches long (4 cm) and has seven pairs of claw-tipped legs. *(Photo by Kenneth P. Sebens)*   zones 2 , 3 , 4

beach hopper, *Orchestia traskiana*   Beach hoppers inhabit driftwood and dead sea-weeds washed up on beaches. Also known as "sand fleas," these tiny crustaceans (amphipods) feed on algae and make tubelike nests from debris. This verdant green species has flat sides and long antennae. It is usually under three-quarters of an inch (2 cm) long. *(Photo by Jak Ayres)*   zones 1 , 2

parasitic crustacean   The flounder in the photograph is the host of a parasitic crustacean of an unidentified species. Parasitism is a common relationship among the sea creatures of the Pacific Northwest. The crustacean will gain its nutrients at the expense of its fish host. *(Photo by Don Bloye)*   zone   5

coon-striped shrimp, *Pandalus danae*   Dark brown and red stripes traverse the white bands along the body of the coon-striped shrimp. This alert shrimp can sometimes be observed on floats. A voracious feeder, it is aggressive towards the larger plankton and small crustaceans. The rostrum is upturned and armed with spines. Its antennae are as long as its body, about five inches (12 cm) when mature. *(Photo by Neil Hurd)*   zone   5

broken-back shrimp, *Heptacarpus*   This shrimp, which grows no longer than two inches (5 cm), may be found among algae in tide pools. The variable brown mottling serves as camouflage while it darts about capturing microscopic animals. It swims backwards by flapping the powerful tail forwards. Female broken-back shrimp carrying eggs under their tails are a common sight in May. *(Photo by Ken Conte)*   zone   5

ghost shrimp, *Callianassa californiensis*   Little piles of sand mark the burrows of this shrimp. It typically inhabits very muddy sand with enough organic material available to form a lining for its burrow. The body is transparent pink and delicate. The ghost shrimp eats small animals and bacteria present in the mud. Its burrows provide homes for many commensals, including worms, crabs, clams, and gobies. The female is usually fat, the male being smaller and thinner. *(Photo by Jak Ayres)*   zones   3 , 4 , 5

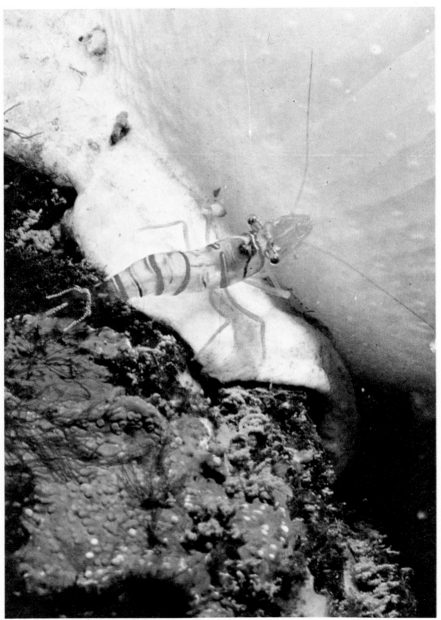

commensal shrimp, *Lebbeus grandimanus* This exotic-looking shrimp lives commensally with the pink anemone, *Cribrinopsis*. The commensal shrimp can be seen on the column of this anemone, perhaps eating mucus the anemone produces. *(Photo by Ronald L. Shimek)* zone 5

Bering hermit crab, *Pagurus beringanus* The Bering hermit is one of the largest intertidal hermit crabs and often occupies moon snail shells. Distinctive orange and white bands are present on its legs and at the base of its pinchers. This crab is a scavenger that wanders the tidal zones searching for larger homes to inhabit and rotting debris to eat. *(Photo by Jak Ayres)* zones 3 , 4 , 5

hairy hermit crab, *Pagurus hirsutiusculus* A scavenger of tide pools, the hairy hermit will sometimes exceed an inch (2.5 cm) in length. Often it is seen in shells too small for it to fit completely into, and if frightened may leave home and scramble away. Common under or between rocks in the intertidal areas, this hairy-appearing hermit crab has light and dark bands on its antennae. *(Photo by Jak Ayres)* zones 3 , 4

tuft-haired crab, *Hapalogaster mertensii*   Hairlike tufts, bristles, and spines cover the red-brown body of this small crab, which is one and a half inches (3 cm) long. One should be careful if handing this creature because the abdomen injures easily. The tuft-haired crab is frequently seen moving slowly along cleaning the bottom of the sea. *(Photo by Dan H. McLachlan)*   zone 4

porcelain crab, *Petrolisthes eriomerus*   Three-quarters of an inch (2 cm) across, the porcelain crab is found under rocks on gravel and sandy beaches. It has long antennae, four pairs of walking legs, large sharp claws, and an extremely flat, round carapace. This crab is thought to be a filter feeder. *(Photo by Jak Ayres)*   zone 4

purple shore crab, *Hemigrapsus nudus*   This active crab exists under most loose rocks on rocky beaches. The crab is reddish or purple with white pinchers. It has a smooth, square carapace that may be an inch and a half across (4 cm). The purple shore crab is able to spend long periods of time out of water while scavenging for dead or living animals. *(Photo by Jak Ayres)*   zones 3 , 4 , 5

northern kelp crab, *Pugettia producta*   The northern kelp crab maintains a clean, smooth, olive green carapace up to four inches (10 cm) long. The two horns dividing the carapace are characteristic of this species. The pinchers are long and strong, but the first pair of walking legs are longer. This crab is common on pilings and among the kelp jungles of Puget Sound. It blends in perfectly with its environment. *(Photo by Dan H. McLachlan)*   zone 5

masked or sharp-nosed crab, *Scyra acutifrons*   The masked crab is slow-moving, but a master of protective disguise. The rough carapace is "planted" with seaweeds, bryozoa, ascidians and sponges, by the crab. Its fairly thick, short legs may be an inch and a half (4 cm) long. *(Photo by Dan H. McLachlan)*   zones 4 , 5

decorator crab, *Oregonia gracilis*   One of the most spidery of the shallow water and piling crabs, the decorator has long slender legs and may be two inches wide (5 cm). This crab actively decorates itself with sponges, bryozoans, seaweeds and other matter, changing its "suit" to blend into new environments. If part of a rock or piling a person is looking at moves, it could be this crab. *(Photo by Dan H. McLachlan)*   zones 4 , 5

dungeness crab, *Cancer magister*   The carapace of the commercially sought dungeness crab commonly measures eight inches (20 cm) wide. Its coloring is somewhat variable, from light browns to dark reds. This crab feeds on small clams and abalones by chipping their shells with its strong pinchers. The pinchers are tipped white. Male and female crabs are easily distinguished by looking at the tails on the undersides of their bodies. The female has a broad tail, which in the summer months holds the egg clusters. *(Photo by Ronald L. Shimek)*   zone   5

red rock crab, *Cancer productus*   The red rock crab is dark brownish red with black tipped pinchers. Abundant in rocky areas and on sandy bottoms among seaweeds, this species is an active hunter feeding on live or dead organic matter. It has a carapace up to six inches (15 cm) wide. *(Photo by Jak Ayres)*   zone   5

Puget Sound king crab, *Lopholithodes mandtii*   This colorful species is orange to scarlet with purple splashes on its spines and ventral side. The dorsal side has four red conelike elevations, the forward one being the largest. If threatened, this unusual crab will tuck its legs under it and resemble a spiny box. It grows up to fifteen pounds (7 kg), and will eat sea stars. *(Photo by Dan H. McLachlan)*   zone   5

galathoid crab, *Munida quadrispina*   This crab actually looks very much like a miniature lobster. It may reach eight inches (20 cm) long and is only seen below the tide lines. The first legs are strong with long pinchers. The galathoid crab swims backwards with its powerful tail. It uses small swimmerets on its abdomen to swim forward. *(Photo by Jak Ayres)*   zone   5

12

CHORDATA: the Chordates, including Sea Squirts
class: Ascidiacea

The phylum Chordata includes fishes, sharks, frogs, snakes, birds, and people. Many of its members are the most developed and the most predatory animals of all, capable of the greatest size, fastest speed, and most adaptive diets. It is also the phylum of the largest brains.

What sets the chordates apart from other animals though, is the fact that they have overcome the problem of support (which the arthropods overcame with exoskeletons) without the shortcomings associated with exoskeletons. To illustrate how important this is for an animal to reach greater dimensions, one only has to remember that the weight of a solid animal increases much faster than its size. For example, if a garden worm were to grow seven feet in diameter, its tissues would not be able to support it and it would sag like a water bed. Each chordate developed a tough, flexible cord of cartilage, called a notochord, down the inside of its back to give this needed support. Running parallel to this ran a central nerve cord. As the chordates developed in complexity and size (as a result of the notochord's superior qualities), the nerve cord slowly merged into the backbone surrounding the notochord until it was completely within it. The notochord was then strengthened by bony calcareous segments or vertebrae that were strung along its length like empty spools of thread along a rope. Besides combining lightweight strength with flexibility, these supportive vertebrae also protected the important nerve cord.

Yet when a person looks at ascidians (sea squirts), which are chordates too, there is no apparent evidence of the chordates' advanced characteristics. When looking inside sea squirts, the same seems to be true. Ascidians look and function more like clams without shells than "vertebrates," and it isn't until one examines their larvae (which resemble the tadpoles of frogs) that the connection is made. It is their larvae that have the nerve cord and supportive notochord in evidence. These characteristics virtually vanish as the animal matures.

Species of ascidians number in the hundreds, and they populate all the oceans of the world from the arctic regions to the greatest depths. And yet, they go relatively unnoticed. Part of the reason for this is that they can be microscopic in size, and at largest are no more than a foot (30 cm) in diameter. Also, they simply appear insignificant.

Ascidians look like small jugs that have two openings. The top hole is the incurrent siphon through which water is pulled into the center of a teardrop-shaped gill or branchial sac that looks and acts very much like a spherical radiator or clam gill. The blood passing through small capillaries in the walls of this branchial sac carries out the gas exchanges of respiration with the water. At the same time, plankton in the water are caught in mucus continually generated from a vertical groove filled with long cilia. This mucus is moved from out of the groove and along the bars of the branchial sac's radiatorlike gridworks by additional cilia which work the mucus into cords. As these cords of mucus move down towards the esophagus at the base of the branchial sac, they become laden with the nutritious plankton.

The excurrent siphon hole is just to the side of the incurrent siphon. From it flows the used water, the ascidian's wastes, and in the case of those which reproduce sexually, the eggs and sperm. (Some species reproduce asexually by a variety of often complex methods of budding to form colonies or compounded forms that may share common excurrent siphons.)

Though the larvae of ascidians look and swim like tadpoles, they soon attach themselves by their heads with an adhesive compound secreted by a special gland, and remain stationary for the duration of their lives. Because they are stationary creatures, ascidians have little need of sense organs and only rely on a concentration of sense organs within the siphons to sample and regulate the flow of water.

Ascidians are covered with a tough, cartilagelike substance to form what is called a tunic. Tunics can vary a great deal among different species and be of various colors and toughnesses. The tunics of ascidians found commonly in the Pacific Northwest waters are usually either "furry," translucent and knobby, or transparent. Whichever, this covering is quite unique because it is made of a cellulose which is the chief constituent of wood and cotton—products of the plant world. Ascidians are the only multicelled animals in the world to produce such a plantlike material, with the exception of mammals—which have cellulose fibers in their skins.

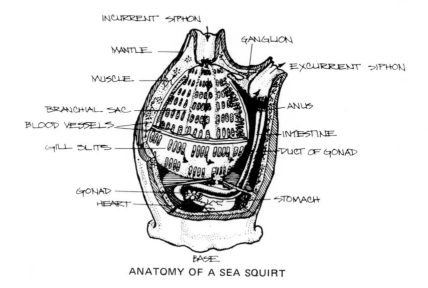

ANATOMY OF A SEA SQUIRT

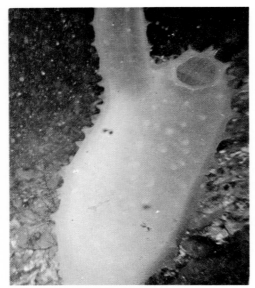

glassy sea squirt, *Ascidia paratropa*   The transparent body of this sea squirt is covered with large glassy tubercles (wartlike projections), is four inches (10 cm) high, and has two siphon openings at the top. The lower siphon draws in the water and suspended food, while the upper siphon is the exhaust. Seen attached to rocks or shells below the tide line, this creature lives only a year. *(Photo by Dan H. McLachlan)* zones 4 , 5

transparent sea squirt, *Corella willmeriana*   This creature looks like a glob of ice at or below the low tide line. It only lives about a year and reaches an inch and a half (3 cm) in height. The organs of the transparent sea squirt are easily observed. Close examination will reveal a sac-shaped heart which pumps blood first in one direction and then the opposite way. *(Photo by Dan H. McLachlan)*   zones 4 , 5

broad-base squirt, *Cnemidocarpa finmarkiensis*   This is an elusive solitary ascidian that usually lives in holes on the floor of Puget Sound. It has a unique, smooth, bright pinkish skin. When extended it is an inch (2.5 cm) high with a base twice that. The siphons appear as crossed folds when the animal is withdrawn, but are round when actively pumping water. Many worms, hydroids, and algae inhabit its base. *(Photo by Dan H. McLachlan)* zones   4 , 5

hairy sea squirt, *Boltenia villosa*   The hairy sea squirt is stalked with a round hairy body. *Boltenia* grows up to two inches (5 cm) high. Its hairs accumulate silt and detritus, giving the yellow body a brown appearance. This solitary ascidian is seen attached to rocks and pilings usually below the low tide zone. *(Photo by Kenneth P. Sebens)*   zones 4 , 5

social ascidian, *Metandrocarpa taylori*   These small ascidians grow only to a quarter inch (6 mm) in width. Lining the undersides of rocks usually below the tideline, they look like masses of red eggs. Careful observation will reveal the two holes of the excurrent and incurrent siphons. Short runners are budded from the parent and develop new individuals (connections are not permanent). Large populations form in this manner. *(Photo by Don Bloye)*   zones 4 , 5

compound ascidian, *Cystodytes*   Compound ascidians are many individuals (zooids) grouped together in a cellulose mass called a tunic. This compound ascidian is grayish or cream colored and appears as a spongelike lump below the tide line. Colonies are formed from a single parent by budding. *(Photo by Dan H. McLachlan)*   zones 5

CHORDATA: class Chondrichthyes

Perhaps no other creatures are feared by people more than snakes and sharks, and of the two, perhaps sharks are feared the most because people feel that, unlike snakes, sharks search them out and attack in a sinister, premeditated way. And there is no denying it, people are victims of shark attacks every year. But it is the authors' opinion, based on their readings and their encounters with sharks in various parts of the world, that sharks have behavior patterns very similar to domestic dogs. Some are openly aggressive and very dangerous; some are not harmful unless their territory is infringed upon; some are harmless unless tormented; some act more aggressive than they really are; and still others are docile and have never been known to attack people. However, for the person who is unfamiliar with sharks, a good rule of thumb is to *calmly* leave the water the moment sharks are sighted unless there is someone present to act as a guide and instructor into shark behavior. Fortunately, people need not fear sharks in Pacific Northwest waters because of the relative scarcity of those species known to attack humans.

The class Chondrichthyes includes all sharks and rays. With the exception of the enormous, filter-feeding whale sharks, which can reach sixty feet (19.4 m), and the large manta rays, which grow as long as seventeen feet (5.2 m) and as wide as twenty feet (6.1 m), sharks and rays are carnivorous predators and, between them, prey on nearly all forms of animal life.

The skeletal structures of sharks and rays contain no true bones but only tough cartilage, such as in the notochord, which partially contains the nerve cord in a groove. Their brains are also sheltered by tough cartilage and resemble loosely-packed clusters of lumps and bulbs. Each of these brain segments is responsible for a different task (one for smell, one for eyes, and so forth), just as portions of more developed animal brains have portions of lobes responsible for individualized body functions.

As predators, sharks and rays have developed some specialized sense organs. Unique among these is a lateral line that runs down both sides of their bodies. These lateral lines are sensory canals that are lined with sensory hairs sensitive to vibrations down to quite low frequencies. Besides the lateral lines, there are pit organs scattered over their heads that also detect vibrations and help determine the direction of their source. These pit organs are pores with sensory hairs in them similar to those found in the lateral lines. Similar in function to the inner ears of people, they work extremely well at identifying abnormalities in fish which are sick or wounded and are therefore easy prey. Sharks and rays also have nostrils for smelling, and they have eyes of varying qualities.

Sharkskin has been used like sandpaper because of the tough placoid scales that cover it. These scales are like minute spines coated with enamel and attached by disc bottoms. Where the shark's flesh rolls over his jaws into his mouth, these placoid scales are enlarged and are his teeth.

Just in back of the mouths of sharks and rays are several parallel splits in the skin that are lined with filaments containing blood vessels. By allowing water to flow in through their mouths and small holes (spiracles) above their eyes and out through these gill slits, they are able to carry out respiration. It used to be thought that sharks could never remain stationary or sleep because of a need for a constant flow of water, but studies are beginning to show that at least some species can remain stationary by perhaps lowering their metabolisms and relying exclusively on their spiracles for current flow.

The Pacific Northwest is the home of seven species of sharks, but the only one that abounds is the spiny dogfish, *Squalus acanthias*. Though the authors have dived in the midst of swarms of these three- and four-foot sharks without a single incident, any animal of that size which sports about with that many teeth should not be treated as harmless. It would be unwise, for instance, to torment them. Also, one should be careful of the two sharp spines protruding from their backs at the leading edges of their two dorsal fins.

Spiny dogfish can live for forty years (Hart 1973). They seem to prefer a single general locality and eat herrings, shrimps, sand lances, smelts, crabs, octopuses, sick or injured salmon (it seems questionable whether or not they pose a threat to healthy salmon), and a variety of other small animals.

Sharks and rays reproduce sexually. A male dogfish will copulate with a female by gripping her with his pelvic fins to hold himself in position. Usually eight or nine young develop from large eggs within the uterus of the female. Like other sharks and rays, they have their place of importance in the oceans. When mature, they help stabilize populations of other marine animals and assist in the development of species by thinning from their numbers the weak and deformed.

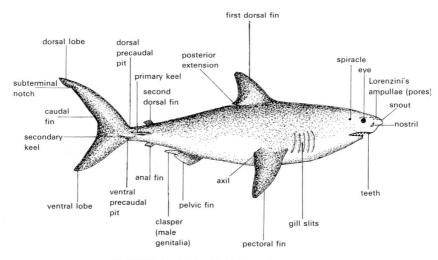

EXTERNAL ANATOMY OF A SHARK

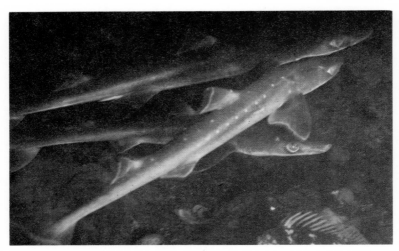

spiny dogfish, *Squalus acanthias*   This abundant shark species has slightly poisonous spines, one in front of each of two dorsal fins. Dogfish seldom exceed four feet (1.2 m) in the Pacific Northwest. They are slate gray or brown above and white beneath, with the young showing irregular rows of light spots on the sides. *Squalus acanthias* has the longest gestation period of any vertebrate, and can live for more than thirty years. *(Photo by Gary Laakso)*   zone 5

big skate, *Raja binoculata*   The big skate prefers sandy bottoms where it feeds on crustaceans and sculpins. The tail on the large, flat symmetrical body has spines, and two obvious spots are located near the base of the fins. On occasion four footers (1.2 m) will loom into view in shallow tidal flats on the incoming tide. *(Photo by Neil Hurd)*   zone 5

ratfish, *Hydrolagus colliei* Unusual-looking, the ratfish's large head tapers to a narrow tail. The skin is smooth and brown, with many whitish spots. Prominent rodentlike teeth are used to eat shellfish and crustaceans, which it seeks out with its keen sense of smell. The ratfish is fairly common. It averages two feet (60 cm) in length, and swims about by flapping its large pectoral fins. *(Photo by Michael A. Kyte)* zone 5

Pacific electric ray, *Torpedo californica* Remarkably round and obvious dorsal fins make it easy to identify the Pacific electric ray. The smooth skin is bluish or brownish with various-sized dark spots. Length is up to three feet (.9 m). If touched in two places, this animal can produce a powerful electric shock. It has been observed feeding on Pacific herring, prefers being partly buried on sandy bottoms, and produces live young. *(Photo by Neil Hurd)* zones 5

CHORDATA: class Osteichthyes

Bony fishes make up the class Osteichthyes, and though there are a few members among them (such as the sturgeons) that still have primarily cartilaginous skeletons, fishes are the first animals to have an endoskeleton made of bone. But there are two other characteristics that set fishes apart from other animals: most have swim or "air" bladders and are usually covered with scales and plates. They are set off from more primitive animals not only by these characterisitcs, but by virtue of the fact that they have more developed and specialized brains and internal organs. In many respects, their anatomies parallel that of humans.

The swim bladder, so unique to fishes, is a bag made of thin membraneous tissue located just under their well-developed vertebral columns. Its function is to adjust the buoyancy of fishes so that they will neither sink nor float from a chosen depth. This is accomplished through the absorption and return of the airlike gas within the bladder from the blood that passes over the surfaces of the membrane. The bladder has taken on the dual task of acting very much like a lung among certain species of fishes that are subjected to shallow water conditions from time to time and must use the atmosphere for their oxygen supply.

Generally speaking, though, fishes breathe with the use of two sets of gills, each of which contains four gill filaments that bear minute plates and capillaries for the purposes of respiration. But unlike sharks, fishes do not need to be in motion to have water pass over their gill filaments. Rather, they pump water over them by pulling water in through their mouths and a one-way oral valve, and then forcing the water out through the gills and gill covers, called operculums, which also act as one-way valves. The mechanics of this is accomplished by the action of the jaw and related skeletal structure, called the visceral skeleton.

Though ages are normally determined through microscopic exam-ination of the growth rings in the ear bones, the ages of those fishes that have scales is marked by microscopic growth rings in the scales. Besides this form of shinglelike exoskeleton, most fishes also have well-developed endoskeletons complete with ribs, a skull (which has a cranium to house the brain and *capsules* for the sense organs associated with sight, smell, and hearing), a jaw, teeth, various supportive bones, bony fin supports that may have lead to the development of legs among amphibians, and finally, a vertebral column that houses the nerve cord.

The fishes of the world can be appreciated for their stunning beauty, complexity, place in the balance of life, and for their importance in the food chain.

If one single thing were to be said about people's general lack of understanding about marine animals, it would be the fact that fishes and most other ocean creatures do not replenish themselves as readily or as easily as most people think. Fishes usually live a long time. It is very common for them to live thirty or forty years. In fact, it's truly remarkable how long many of the ocean's animals do live. Ultimately, what this means is that harvesting the sea must be done with wisdom and respect. The taking of most life represents such a vast depletion in numbers of a given species that the impact is far greater and more complex than the average person can presently fully comprehend. The marine world is a house of cards with the fishes at the top and the world of the planktons at the bottom. Each in one way or another depends on the other for its existence, and when one species suffers, all suffer.

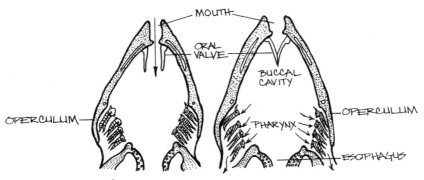

THE GILL AERATING SYSTEM AMONG FISHES

steelhead trout, *Salmo gairdneri*   The steelhead trout is metallic green or blue dorsally and has silver shading along the sides. Dark spots mark the back, dorsal, and tail fins. A large fish, sea-run steelhead average twelve pounds (5.5 kg). Key features include a short head with no trace of red under the lower jaw, and ten to thirteen anal rays. After spawning in fresh water, the sea-run steelhead venture to the sea at least once. Those that remain in lakes or streams are called rainbow or kamloops trout, a fact that adds confusion to an already hard group to identify. *(Photo courtesy of the Washington State Department of Fisheries)*   zone   5

cutthroat trout, *Salmo clarki*   This trout is named for the red marks under its jaw. The back is greenish-blue, the sides are silvery, and there are many black dots spotting the back, sides, and fins. The cutthroat lives both in salt and fresh water. Sea-run fish will weigh four pounds (1.8 kg) and non-migratory individuals up to forty-one pounds (20 kg). *(Photo courtesy of the Washington State Department of Fisheries)*   zone   5

chinook salmon, *Oncorhynchus tshawytscha*   Recorded up to one hundred and twenty-six pounds (55 kg), the chinook is the largest of Pacific salmon. Common names are king, spring, tyee, or blackmouth. The inside of the mouth of this species is black with loose set teeth. It will live three, four, or even seven years. Diet consists of herrings, squids, and any other small fishes or crustaceans available. *(Photo courtesy of the Washington State Department of Fisheries)* zone   5

coho or silver salmon, *Oncorhynchus kisutch*   Coho or silver salmon have firmly set teeth on white gums, plus spots on their backs and the upper halves of their tail fins. They live three years. After less than one year in fresh water, they migrate to the sea. When mature, they return to the "home" stream where they spawn and die. The coho is essentially a fish eater, but will dine on most anything that moves which is small enough to eat. It will weigh up to thirty-one pounds (14 kg). *(Photo courtesy of the Washington State Department of Fisheries)*   zone   5

pink or humpback salmon, *Oncorhynchus gorbuscha*   The pink salmon has small scales and large oval blotches on its back and tail. This salmon lives only two years. The young migrate to salt water soon after hatching in streams. Mature males turn reddish and become humpbacked; the females are olive green with dark stripes. The average weight is around five pounds (2.5 kg). *(Photo courtesy of the Washington State Department of Fisheries)*   zone   5

chum or dog salmon (immature), *Oncorhynchus keta*   A large pupil and the presence of black edges on the pectoral, anal, and tail fins mark this usually eight- to eighteen-pound (4-8 kg) salmon. It hatches in fresh-water streams, journeys to sea, and returns three to five years later to spawn and die. The mature fish has dusky bars across its sides. *(Photo courtesy of the Washington State Department of Fisheries)*   zone   5

sockeye salmon, *Oncorhynchus nerka*   The sockeye salmon, commonly called the red or blueback salmon, has a greenish-blue back with many small speckles. Mature spawning adults sport green heads and rich red sides; females are less brilliant. The young make their way to lakes after hatching and remain a year or more—sometimes becoming landlocked. They will live three to six years but usually mature at four years, returning to the same lake or river they were born in, to mate and then die. Sockeye feed on small crustaceans and grow to fifteen pounds (7 kg). *(Photo courtesy of the Washington State Department of Fisheries)*   zone   5

Pacific herring, *Clupea harengus*   The Pacific herring is a common fish preyed upon by almost all predatory fishes, sea birds, and marine mammals. It has silvery scales, a forked tail, large lower jaw bone, and single dorsal fin. The average adult is ten inches (25 cm) long. A single female may produce twenty thousand eggs, which are fertilized externally, sometimes in massive spawning areas. Often the young are observed in huge schools, called "herring balls," in tight formation near the surface. *(Photo by Jak Ayres)*   zone   5

surf smelt, *Hypomesus pretiosus*   A reflecting line marks the silvery sides of this greenish-backed fish. It averages about six inches (15 cm) and has a squared off adipose and forked tail fin. The surf smelt can be seen spawning on sandy beaches between waves. It eats a wide variety of small crustaceans and in turn is eaten by many larger creatures. *(Photo by Jak Ayres)*   zone   5

Pacific cod, *Gadus macrocephalus*   Usually found in depths of one hundred feet or more, the Pacific cod is characterized by three dorsal fins and a long chin barbel. It is brown to gray with many spots on the back and sides. This fish grows quickly and may live ten years, reaching three feet (.9 m) in length. *(Photo by Michael A. Kyte; courtesy of Point Defiance Aquarium)*   zone   5

Pacific tomcod, *Microgadus proximus*   This light brown to green fish can be seen around shallow sandy bottoms. It has a pointed first dorsal fin, with all fins black-tipped. The whiskerlike chin barbels are small on a receding lower jaw. Rarely over a foot in length (30 cm), the tomcod is the smallest of the Pacific Northwest's true cods. It eats shrimps and small crustaceans. *(Photo by Michael A. Kyte; courtesy of the Point Defiance Aquarium)* zone   5

lingcod, *Ophiodon elongatus*   The lingcod is a long, large-headed greenling usually light green or brown with dark mottling. The long dorsal fin has one moderate notch. The mouth is big with large teeth. From December to March males brood over masses of pinkish-white eggs. These males should be given a wide berth as they can be quite protective. This fish feeds on smaller fishes, various crustaceans, and octopuses. It may be observed from just below the tide line to well below one hundred feet (30 m). Some lingcod have reached six feet (1.8 m). They can weigh over eighty pounds (36 kg) and can live thirty-five years. *(Photo by Gary Laakso)*   zone   5

kelp greenling, *Hexagrammos decagrammus*   Usually under twenty inches (50 cm) in length, the kelp greenling is a beautiful fish with distinctive color patterns. The brownish-olive male has bright blue spots on its head, while the female is light brown to gold with brown flecks over most of her back and sides. It prefers rocky areas and eats almost anything, even sea anemones. *(Photo by Tony Lucas)*   zone   5

painted greenling, *Oxylebius pictus*   Seven dark, reddish, vertical bars mark the gold to tan body of the painted greenling. The head of this species is elongated and almost pointed. The length may reach ten inches (25 cm). This fish is often seen lying motionless on the sides of rocks, upside down on cave roofs, or in other unique positions. *(Photo by Dan H. McLachlan)*   zone   5

rock sole, *Lepidopsetta bilineata* When flatfish are observed with the ventral fin pointing downward, then both eyes and the darker colored side are either on the right side or the left side. The rock sole's eyes are on the right. A lateral line arches over the pectoral fin. Capable of camouflage, they are variable in color, usually being mottled brown or gray. They are about 20 inches (50 cm) long, and can often be seen combing the bottom for mollusc siphons, worms, and crustaceans. *(Photo by Michael A. Kyte)* zone 5

English sole, *Parophrys vetulus* The English sole is commonly seen in shallow water in the spring, but moves deeper in the winter. It has a pointed head and snout. The body is shades of brown with a lateral line that does not arch over the pointed pectoral fin. Length is up to 22 inches (56 cm). It eats clams, clam siphons, brittle stars, and crustaceans. *(Photo by Larry A. Martin)* zones 4 , 5

c-o sole, *Pleuronichthys coenosus*   The dark brown c-o sole has a conspicuous black spot in the middle of its body and sometimes on the tail fin. The eyes of this fish are usually positioned on the right side. It may reach fourteen inches (35 cm) in length. The eggs are cast to the currents. Young prefer the shallows, while the adults move into deep water. They eat most anything found on the bottom. *(Photo by Michael A. Kyte)*   zone   5

starry flounder, *Platichthys stellatus*   This common flatfish of the shallows has prominent bars of alternating shades on the fins. Eyes develop on either side of the olive green or brown body. It may weigh twenty pounds (9.1 kg) and reach over three feet (.9 m) in length. *(Photo by Pat Siedlack; courtesy of the Seattle Aquarium)*   zone   5

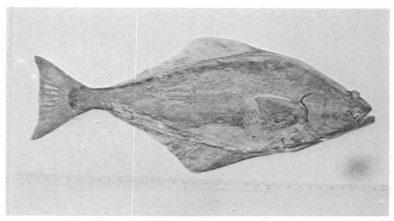

Pacific halibut, *Hippoglossus stenolepis* This fish of the ocean floor may reach four hundred pounds (181 kg), the female being the larger. The young fish begin life below one hundred fathoms and migrate to the shallows, where they settle to the bottom and begin to lie on their left side. At this time the left eye moves over the top of the head to a position next to the right eye. As the fish matures, it moves again to deeper waters. Halibuts eat squids, octopuses, fishes, crabs, clams, and other life forms found in the murky depths. *(Photo courtesy of the Washington State Department of Fisheries)* zone 5

striped seaperch, *Embiotoca lateralis* A common piling and cliff dweller, this tropical-looking fish displays fifteen brilliant blue horizontal stripes on a copper-colored body. It eats crustaceans, mussels, worms, and eggs. The striped seaperch is a schooling fish with an elaborate mating ritual. The young are born live during the summer months. They grow to about fifteen inches (37 cm). *(Photo by Michael A. Kyte)* zone 5

shiner seaperch, *Cymatogaster aggregata*   Three vertical yellow bars, a shining body, and dark longitudinal bars allow for field identification of the shiner seaperch (the yellow shiner). Up to six inches in length (15 cm), it is an active, early morning feeder that nips the appendages off barnacles, mussels, and algae. The young are born alive, tail first, in June or July. *(Photo by Bob Turner)*   zone 5

pile seaperch, *Rhacochilus vacca*   A silver body with dusky bars, a black cheek spot, and a deeply notched tail fin mark the pile seaperch. This fish averages fourteen inches (35 cm) in length and lives in schools along rocky shores and pilings. An avid mussel eater, it crushes the mussels' shells and gobbles up the pieces. *(Photo by Jak Ayres; courtesy of the Seattle Aquarium)*   zone 5

copper rockfish, *Sebastes caurinus*   This rockfish frequents shallow waters. It is usually brownish green with copper patches on the sides. Mature length of the copper is about twenty-one inches (52 cm). *(Photo by Don Bloye)*   zone   5

black rockfish, *Sebastes melanops*   Basslike, the black rockfish is seen off rocky shores, sometimes schooling well above the bottom—even leaping like trout for flies. It is black on the back, blending to silver-gray with black mottling on the sides. This species may reach twenty-four inches (60 cm) in length. *(Photo by Gary Laakso)*   zone   5

quillback rockfish, *Sebastes maliger*   The dorsal fin of the quillback is long and light-streaked, while the body is usually shades of brown and yellow. This fish lives both in shallow, rocky areas and in deeper waters. Individuals may be twenty-one inches (61 cm) long, and live over twenty years. The scientific name means "magnificent mast bearer," referring to the tail dorsal spines. The spines of all rockfishes are tipped with a painful toxin and should be avoided. *(Photo by Larry Moulton)*   zone   5

china rockfish, *Sebastes nebulosus*   This rockfish is hard to mistake with its blue-black body and striking yellow markings. It prefers moderate depths and remains close to a home crevice. The same rockfish may be observed in its favorite spot year after year. It grows to almost seventeen inches (43 cm). *(Photo by Don Bloye)*   zone   5

brown rockfish, *Sebastes auriculatus*   The brown rockfish is especially common in Puget Sound. It sports two shades of brown in blotchy patterns, and has dusky pinks or yellows on the lower parts of its head. A large one will reach up to twenty-one inches (52 cm). *(Photo by Michael A. Kyte)*   zone   5

yellowtail rockfish, *Sebastes flavidus*   This streamlined fish can be seen in schools off the bottom in the Strait of Juan de Fuca. It is olive green with brownish hues and the fins are dusky green to yellow. The yellowtail rockfish eats small fishes and crustaceans, and grows to twenty-six inches (65 cm). *(Photo by Michael A. Kyte)*   zone   5

yelloweye rockfish or red snapper, *Sebastes ruberrimus*   This fish is sometimes seen by sport divers, but usually lives at a depth of twenty-five to three hundred fathoms (46 to 550 m). It is orange-yellow, marked with some black mottling around the head. Eyes are brilliant yellow and the fin tips, black. The yelloweye rockfish reaches 3 feet (91 cm) in length. It eats crustaceans and small fishes from the deep reefs along the Pacific coast. *(Photo by William L. High)*   zone   5

canary rockfish, *Sebastes pinniger*   This is a colorful, common rockfish. It is orange with three bright orange stripes across the face and some gray mottling on the dorsal side. The canary rockfish is seen below one hundred feet (30.5 m) and occurs to depths of two hundred fathoms (366 m). It may be thirty inches (76 cm) long. *(Photo by William L. High)*   zone   5

tiger rockfish, *Sebastes nigrocinctus*   Divers that venture below one hundred feet (30.5 m) often see this solitary rockfish in cracks and caves. The tiger rockfish is often light colored with five vertical dark red-brown bars across its body and two dark red-brown bars radiating from the eyes. This fish may be twenty-four inches (61 cm) long. It is aggressive, territorial, and becomes darker when disturbed. *(Photo by William L. High)*   zone 5

cabezon, *Scorpaenichthys marmoratus*   Reaching thirty inches (75 cm) and weighing over twenty-five pounds (11 kg), the cabezon is a large member of the sculpin family. The large head has three spines near the mouth. The body is scaleless and has a mottled appearance of varying greens, browns, or grays. Greenish eggs are laid on rocks near the low tide line from January to March. The cabezon eats crustaceans and small fishes. *(Photo by William L. High)*   zone 5

red Irish lord, *Hemilepidotus hemilepidotus*   This thickset fish is brick red mottled with brown, white, orange, black, or, sometimes, brilliant red. The band of scales surrounding the dorsal fin is a good field check for identification. A bottom dweller, the red Irish lord feeds on crabs, barnacles, and mussels. It is a master at camouflage and may reach twenty inches (50 cm). *(Photo by Dan H. McLachlan)*   zone   5

sailfin sculpin, *Nautichthys oculofasciatus*   This remarkable sculpin has five tall spines on the dorsal fin and a striking dark band through the eye and across the cheek, making for an easy identification. Approximately six inches (15 cm) long, the body is a variable, pale color. The sailfin can be seen grazing for crustaceans among mussel beds or resting upside down on the roofs of caves. *(Photo by Larry Moulton)*   zone   5

grunt sculpin, *Rhamphocottus richardsoni* This three-inch (7.6 cm) bodied large-headed sculpin grunts when frightened. It swims in a curious head-up manner or crawls across the bottom using its pectoral fins. The grunt sculpin seems to enjoy rocky, shallow areas where it moves about using its long snout to poke into holes or among barnacles for worms and other animals. *(Photo by Dan H. McLachlan)* zones 4 , 5

Pacific staghorn sculpin, *Leptocottus armatus* The Pacific staghorn sculpin was so named because of the antlerlike spines on its gill covers. A black spot on the spiny dorsal fin is also a prominent characteristic. This scaleless sculpin grows to a foot and a half (45 cm) in length and often buries itself in the sand with only the eyes peering out. It feeds on small crustaceans and other fishes in shallows and tide pools. *(Photo by Jak Ayres; courtesy of the Seattle Aquarium)* zones 3 , 4 , 5

buffalo sculpin, *Enophrys bison*   The buffalo sculpin dwells on the bottom in shallow water. It has a blunt head with small eyes and a long spine at the top of each gill cover. When disturbed, these spines make it a formidable looking foot-long (30.5 cm) creature. The diet of this sculpin includes small fishes, crustaceans, mussels, and sea lettuce *(Ulva)*. *(Photo by Dan H. McLachlan)*   zone 5

great sculpin, *Myoxocephalus polyacanthocephalus*   The great sculpin may be over two feet (61 cm) long. It can be distinguished from the cabazon by the long, straight spine which projects from the operculum (gill cover) and by the scales upon its head. This sculpin is mostly olive green with four broad dark bands across its back. A common inhabitant of moderate depths, it preys mostly on small fishes. *(Photo by Dan H. McLachlan)*   zone 5

roughback sculpin, *Chitonotus pugetensis*   This brownish-green sculpin may be 9 inches (23 cm) long. It has an easily recognizable dorsal fin that is deeply notched between the third and fourth spine. The upper head is covered with rough scales. During the day the roughback sculpin may be seen in shallow waters buried in the mud or sand, at night it feeds on shrimps and other small crustaceans. *(Photo by Michael A. Kyte)*   zones 4 , 5

tide pool sculpin, *Oligocottus maculosus*   This is one of the most common sculpins in tide pools and along rocky shores. It has spots on the base of the tail, and is less than three inches (8 cm) long. Depending on its environment, the tide pool sculpin may be blackish, red, brown, or green, blending to cream on its belly. Behavioral scientists have moved this fish and found that it tends to return to its home tide pool. *(Photo by Jak Ayres)*   zones   4 , 5

sturgeon poacher, *Agonus acipenserinus*   The sturgeon poacher has large pectoral fins, shiny plates along its sides, a bottom-facing mouth, and clusters of whiskerlike cirri, which hang from its flattish snout. It sweeps the bottom in search of worms and small crustaceans. Large for a poacher, the well-named sturgeon poacher grows to a foot (30.5 cm) in length. *(Photo by Dan H. McLachlan)*   zone   5

Pacific spiny lumpsucker, *Eumicrotremus orbis*   The stocky, clumsy-looking Pacific spiny lumpsucker has cone-shaped scales of many different sizes. Its ventral fins are modified into an adhesive disc. This fish is a slow, wavering swimmer and uses its disc to attach to rocks during heavy currents. During February, the male of this species guards the eggs. The Pacific spiny lumpsucker reaches a maximum length of five inches (13 cm). *(Photo by Larry Moulton)*   zone   5

threespine stickleback, *Gasterosteus aculeatus* This small four-inch (10 cm) fish can be found in both fresh and salt waters, but in salt water it appears to have thicker scales and to be larger than the fresh-water animal. The threespine stickleback is territorial. The male of this species establishes boundaries, makes nests, and even guards and cares for the eggs until they are hatched. *(Photo by Jak Ayres)* zone 5

pipefish, *Syngnathus griseolineatus* This relative of the sea horse camouflages itself in shallow beds of eelgrass. It is covered by bony plates, has a tiny mouth and tail, and may be a foot (31 cm) long. After an intriguing courtship, the female places the eggs into the brood pouch of the male. The pipefish swims by rapidly moving its dorsal fins. Interesting to observe, it moves along slowly, slurping up microscopic life. *(Photo by Pat Siedlak; courtesy of the Seattle Aquarium)* zone 5

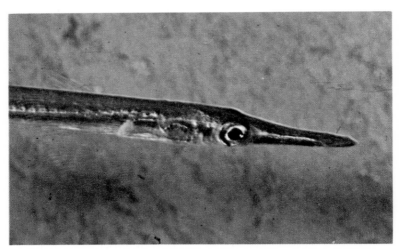

tube-snout, *Aulorhynchus flavidus*   The slender tube-snout has many spines on its back. This fish is often seen singly or in schools lunging for small swimming organisms and snapping them up with its small mouth. *(Photo by Pat Siedlak; courtesy of the Seattle Aquarium)*   zones   4 , 5

crested goby, *Coryphopterus nicholsi*   The crested goby, often,called the blackeye goby, is seen in tide pools and among rocky, underwater rubble. It is a light orange or tanish brown with black eyes, and can easily be identified by the black edge showing on the front dorsal fin. This five-inch (12 cm) territorial fish, often seen peering out from its lair under rocks, feeds on small crustaceans and larvae. *(Photo by Dan H. McLachlan)*   zones
4 , 5

snake prickleback, *Lumpenus sagitta* The snake prickleback has a narrow body approximately eighteen inches (45 cm) in length. Usually seen at night, this fish can be easily recognized by its elongated dorsal fin and by the horizontal barring along its sides. Invertebrates such as worms and crustaceans compose its diet. *(Photo by Bob Turner)* zones 4 , 5

northern clingfish, *Gobiesox maeandricus* The northern clingfish is seen at low tide on overturned rocks where it solidly attaches itself by an adhesive sucker disc, a modification on the anal and pectoral fins. This fish is usually about four inches (10 cm) long. It eats small molluscs and crustaceans. *(Photo by Jak Ayres)* zones 4 , 5

plainfin midshipman, *Porichthys notatus*   This flatheaded fish has protruding eyes. The males are seen in shallow waters during spring and summer, partially buried in the sand or under rocks, guarding the eggs. The plainfin midshipman has two interesting abilites: it is sometimes known as the singing fish because of the melodic sounds it makes; and it has many rows of luminous organs (photophores), which look like a midshipman's naval uniform and can be flashed at will. *(Photo by Dan H. McLachlan)*   zone   5

mosshead warbonnet, *Chirolophis nugator*   When looking under rocks near the low tide line or in shallow areas, one may see the decorated head of the mosshead warbonnet. It has many even-sized growths, called cirri, on top of its head, and a row of round dark spots evenly spaced on the elongated dorsal fin. This warbonnet may be five inches (13 cm) long, and of variable color. *(Photo by Dan H. McLachlan)*   zones   4 , 5

crescent gunnel, *Pholis laeta* About ten inches (25 cm) long, this eel-like fish has many crescent markings along its dorsal fin and body. The crescent gunnel is seen in tide pools, deep in holes, and among rocks. It eats small organisms and seems to prefer areas abundant with seaweeds. *(Photo by Dan H. McLachlan)* zones 4 , 5

penpoint gunnel, *Apodichthys flavidus* The penpoint gunel is one of several fishes found among rocks in shallow waters. Often seen in pairs, it can be easily identified by the dark lines running vertically below its eyes. Individuals may reach eighteen inches (46 cm) in length and appear in a variety of colors. A large penlike spine protrudes from the anal opening, which explains the name of this gunnel. *(Photo by Dan H. McLachlan)* zones 4 , 5

wolfeel, *Anarrhichthys ocellatus*   Young wolfeels are more streamlined than adults and are distinguished by orange, gold, and black markings. Wolfeel jaws are strong and the teeth are sharp for crushing and eating shelled invertebrates like crabs, clams, and sea urchins. *(Photo by Don Bloye)*   zone   5

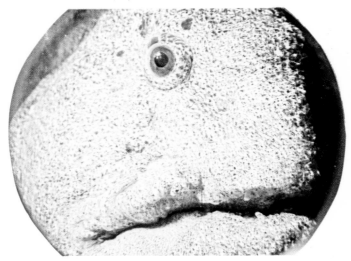

wolfeel, *Anarrhichthys ocellatus*   Adult wolfeels look remarkably fierce with their small eyes, big gaping mouths, large teeth, and thick lips. They are timid creatures that enjoy the comfort of caves/lairs and can be seen living in pairs. A gentle mother, the female encircles her eggs and does not leave them until they hatch. Some adults reach eight feet in length (2.4 m). In relation to body size, the male has a larger head and thicker lips than the female. Wolfeels have been found in shallow rocky areas as well as in water over one hundred fathoms deep. *(Photo by Don Bloye)*   zone   5

GLOSSARY

abdomen. The belly.

aboral. The side opposite the mouth, such as the top side of sand dollars.

adductor. A muscle that draws two things together.

alternation of generations. Also called metagenesis, this phenomenon is part of the reproductive cycle of certain animals—such as some hydroids—in which both sexual and asexual means are employed.

anatomy. The physical structure of plants and animals.

Annelida. The phylum of the segmented worms.

anterior. The front end of an animal.

Anthozoa. The class of sea anemones, sea pens, sea whips, and cup coral.

anus. The posterior opening of the digestive tract, through which solid waste is excreted.

Aristotle's lantern. The tough kind of five-toothed jaw in sea urchins.

Arthropoda. The phylum of crabs, shrimps, lobsters, barnacles, insects, spiders, scorpions, ticks, centipedes, and millipedes.

Ascidiacea. The class of chordates that includes the sea squirts.

asexual reproduction. The method by which animals multiply without benefit of sperm and eggs but through budding or fission.

auditory. The sense of hearing.

auricularia. The larvae in the reproductive cycle of certain holothuroids.

autonomy. Independence and completeness.

autotomy. The ability of certain animals to shed an appendage or part of their bodies when survival demands it.

avicularium. A nipperlike zoöid that is part of some bryozoans and is thought to provide some protection.

bilateral symmetry. A structural design which can be divided into two identical halves.

bivalves. Two shells like those that clams have protecting them. Also, members of the class Bivalvia.

Bivalvia. The class comprised of clams, mussels, oysters, scallops, pectens, and geoducks.

bladder. A thin sac or bag for holding gases or fluids.

Brachiopoda. The phylum of the lamp shells.

branchial. Gills, as in the gill sacs of ascidians.

brood pouches. A body cavity in some animals in which their young may develop before release into the elements.

Bryozoa. A phylum of microscopic "moss animals" that make colonies of a wide variety of forms.

budding. An asexual method of reproduction by which a small portion of an adult animal pulls away to become its offspring.

byssus. Silky threads used by some molluscs to attach themselves to the substrate.

Calcarea. A class of sponges that are supported by hard calcareous structures.

calcareous. Containing calcium carbonate.

carbonate of lime. A hard, chalklike substance ($CaCO_3$).

carnivore. A plant or animal that eats animals.

cellulose. The chief material in the walls of plant cells and ascidians.

Cephalopoda. The class of molluscs that includes octopuses, nautiluses, and squids.

cerata. The featherlike projections on certain nudibranchs. Respiration occurs through the surfaces of the cerata.

chiton. Tough, horny material that makes up a part of the exoskeletons of arthropods.

choanocytes. Cells that have fine flagella extending from them to help create water current, and which feed on plankton and absorb oxygen from water drawn through small collared openings at the base of each hair.

Chondrichthyes. The class of chordates that includes sharks and rays.

Chordata. The phylum of ascidians, fishes, sharks, frogs, snakes, birds, people, and other animals with backbones.

chromatophores. Pigmentation cells capable of changing color at will.

cilia. Small flagellating "hairs" that create motion by their whiplike movements.

ciliated chambers. Cavities such as are found in sponges, which are lined with cells that have fine flagella extending from them to help create water current.

circulatory system. A system of organs and tissues involved in pushing liquids, such as blood, throughout an animal's body.

cloacal chamber. An enlargement of the hind gut of sea cucumbers, from which respiratory trees branch.

Cnidaria. The phylum of hydroids, jellyfishes, sea anemones, sea pens, sea whips, and cup coral.

colloblasts. These are glue cells that secrete an adhesive material to entangle prey.

colony. A group of plants or animals of the same kind living or growing together in close association.

columella muscle. The muscle which pulls certain gastropods within their protective shells.

commensal. The relationship between two or more animals in which they live and feed together without helping or harming each other.

communal. Living together harmoniously in the same area.

corpuscle. A cell such as a blood cell.

coupling. The physical joining or linking of two animals for the purposes of reproduction.

cranium. The part of a vertebrate's skull that houses the brain.

Crustacea. The class of crabs, shrimps, lobsters, and barnacles.

Ctenophora. The phylum of the combjellies.

cuticle. The exoskeleton of an arthropod.

cuvierian organs. White, very sticky tubes that are cast out by certain sea cucumbers as a means of entangling their attackers.

diatom. One-celled, microscopic algae with cell walls made of silica.

dioecious. Having either male or female sex organs in separate, individual animals.

dorsal. The upper or back side of an animal.

Echinodermata. The phylum of spiny-skinned animals such as sea stars and sea urchins.

Echinoidea. The class of sea urchins and sand dollars.

egg. The reproductive germ cell or gamete produced by the female gonad of an animal.

endoskeleton. The internal supporting framework of certain animals.

enviseration. The rupturing out of internal organs of certain sea cucumbers when attacked.

epicuticle. The new cuticle or exoskeleton formed under the old in molting arthropods.

epidermis. The outermost layer of skin.

esophagus. A tube that connects the mouth with the stomach in many animals.

excurrent pores. Called oscula, these are the large openings on the surfaces of sponges.

exoskeleton. The tough outer covering of arthropods, molluscs, and brachiopods.

fertilization. The union of sperm with eggs in the reproductive process of all animals which reproduce sexually.

flagella. Long, hairlike extensions capable of vigorous, thrashing movements. Found on certain protozoans and flame cells.

flagellate. To whip back and forth.

flame cells. Cells equipped with flagella specializing in excreting waste.

follicle. A small cavity or sac within the body of an animal.

gametes. Mature reproductive cells of either sex. If male, it is called sperm; if female, it is called egg.

ganglia. Clusters of nerve cells or nerve centers.

Gastropoda. The class of snails, slugs, whelks, nudibranchs, limpets, and abalones.

gemmules. An asexually formed glob of cells capable of enduring severe conditions to form into an image of its parent (sponge) when conditions improve.

gills. A series of plates or feathery filaments through which respiration occurs in some animals.

girdle. Among chitons a tough, leathery border into which their plates are set.

gonad. The sex organ of either the male or female animal.

gustatory. The sense of taste.

herbivore. An animal that feeds on vegetable matter.

hinge teeth. The pivots that align the shells of bivalves.

Holothuroidea. The class of sea cucumbers and gherkins.

hydraulic. Using liquid such as water to operate moving parts.

hydroids. see Hydrozoa.

Hydrozoa. A class of cnidarians that are generally made up of colonies of polyps, called zoöids, and may look like small, dusty ferns.

hypodermis. The outermost layer of skin of arthropods that secretes the exoskeleton.

incurrent canals. Called ostia, these are the small, porelike openings on the surfaces of sponges.

intertidal. The area between the high water mark and the low water mark.

intestine. The lower, tubular portion of the digestive tract between the stomach and the anus of many kinds of animals.

invertebrate. An animal lacking a backbone.

labial palps. Fleshy lips such as are around the mouths of bivalves.

larva. The juvenile stage in the development of many animals.

lithocysts. The balance organs of such animals as jellyfishes.

lophophore. A ring of tentacles that encircle the mouths of certain animals.

madreporite filter. A flexible calcareous plate in echinoderms that filters the water used in their hydraulic systems.

mantle. A thick layer of flesh among molluscs, which may secrete a protective shell.

manubrium. In jellyfishes, the stalklike projection hanging from the center of their mantles.

medusa. A jellyfishlike stage in the development of certain anthozoans.

mesogloea. The gelatinous material between the inner and outer body walls of animals, such as in polyps.

metabolism. The total chemical and physical process by which energy is made available for the life functions of animals.

metagenesis. See "alternation of generations."

metazoa. Multicelled animals.

Mollusca. The phylum of chitons, tusk shells, clams, oysters, snails, slugs, nudibranchs, squids, and octopuses.

monoecious. Describes an animal that has both male and female sex organs. Also referred to as hermaphroditic.

multivalves. When there are more than two shells that provide protection as with certain molluscs such as chitons.

nacre. The inner, mother-of-pearl layer of shell of certain molluscs, especially bivalves.

nematocysts. Stinging cells.

Nemertea. The phylum of the ribbon worms.

nephridium. A kidney or tubular excretory organ found in many invertebrates.

notochord. A primitive sort of spinal column that is a tough, flexible rod of cartilagelike material.

olfactory. The sense of smell.

operculum. A lid or cover such as the gill covers of fishes or the plate which closes the opening in the shells of many gastropods when the animal retracts itself.

optic nerve. Nerves made up of sensory fibers that carry visual data from the retina of an eye to the brain.

oscula. The large excurrent pores on the surfaces of sponges.

osphradium. A chemosensory organ in the siphons of bivalves and gastropods that tests the quality of incoming water.

ossicles. Microscopic limy plates just under the skin of holothuroids that provide limited protection.

Osteichthyes. The class of bony fish.

ostia. The small incurrent pores on the surfaces of sponges.

ovicells. Hollow cells in which the fertile eggs of certain zoöids develop into larvae.

ovoviviparous. Animals which keep their eggs within themselves until they have hatched, but without placental attachment.

pallial groove. Among chitons, the groove just under the edge of their girdles in which their gills are located.

papilla. A fleshy projection of the body wall.

parasite. An organism that lives at the expense of another species.

pedal disc. The structure by which certain animals such as sea anemones attach themselves to the substrate; also known as "basal disc."

pedicellariae. Specialized spines that keep the other spines on sea urchins free of entangling debris.

periostracum. The protective outer layer of molluscan shells.

perismatic layer. The thick middle layer of molluscan shells.

peristalsis. A rhythmic, wavelike set of muscle contractions for the purpose of moving material such as in an intestine.

pharynx. The part of the digestive tract between the lips and the esophagus. In some animals this is also the gill region.

phylum. The largest groupings of living things for reasons of classification.

photophores. The luminous organ found in certain animals.

photosensitive. Is stimulated by light.

pit organ. Special pores equipped with sensory hairs that detect vibrations.

placoid. Platelike, such as the toothy scales on sharkskin.

plankton. A general name for the small organisms suspended and drifting in bodies of water.

planulae. The larval stage in the reproductive cycle of some cnidarians.

Platyhelminthes. The phylum that includes the flatworms.

pluteus. The free-swimming larval stage in the reproductive cycle of sea urchins and sand dollars.

polyp. A sessile (attached) cnidarian.

polypide. The living portion of zoöids.

Polyplacophora. The class of chitons.

Porifera. The phylum of sponges.

posterior. The end of an animal away from the head such as the hindquarter or rear.

predator. An animal which preys on another.

proboscis. A long, flexible, elongated sensory organ or snout.
progeny. The descendant or offspring of an animal.
protophyta. One-celled plants.
protoplasm. A colorless, translucent, semifluid substance which is considered the living matter of all cells and tissue.

radial symmetry. A structural design that is circular and spokelike and has a central axis.
radula. A rasplike tongue covered with chitinous teeth which many molluscs use in obtaining food.
regeneration. The development of new parts to replace those lost through amputation or rejection. Also, another word for reproduction.
rhopalium. The statoliths of certain jellyfishes.
rostrum. The beaklike projection from the heads of certain animals.

Scyphozoa. A class of cnidarians commonly called jellyfishes, which are distinguishable by the visible presence of their gonads.
scyphistoma. A stage in the reproductive cycle of scyphozoans. They look like sea anemones or stacks of upside down jellyfishes.
sea anemone. A flowerlike animal that is a cnidarian and can be considered a jellyfish that has become stationary.
sexual reproduction. The method by which animals multiply through the union of eggs and sperm.
siphon. A tube to transport liquid.
spaeridia. The sensory tube feet on the surfaces of some echinoderms such as sea urchins and sand dollars.
spat. Ciliated larvae that are part of the reproductive cycles of some bivalves.
sperm or spermatozoid. The reproductive cell or gamete produced by the male gonad of certain animals.
spicules. A rod or narrow supporting structure made of silica or carbonate of lime and coming in a variety of shapes; found in sponges, hydroids, and nudibranchs.
spiracle. A breathing hole.
sponge. The simplest form of multicellular animal life.
spongin. A rather tough protein fiber that gives support to noncalcareous sponges.
statolith. A simple sense organ which helps certain animals determine an upright position.
stomach. A saclike enlargement of the digestive tract of many animals where food is stored, diluted, and broken down for digestion.
strobila. A stage in the reproductive cycle of certain scyphozoans.

substrate. The base or material upon which an animal lives, such as sand, rock, mud, or clay.

symbiotic. The relationship in which two or more animals live and eat together and by doing so, help each other.

tactile. The sense of touch.

test. The hard skeleton of sea urchins or sand dollars, from which the spines or tunic and feet extend.

tubercle. A swelling, bump, or small rounded projection.

tunic. Among ascidians, the tough, cartilagelike outer covering.

valve. The shell of such animals as clams and brachiopods.

ventral. The lower (or stomach) side of an animal.

verrucae. Small, flat, wartlike protuberances, such as on beaded sea anemones and other animals.

vertebrate. An animal having a backbone.

vibracula. Hairlike reduced zoöids which are thought to provide some protection for certain bryozoans.

viscera. The internal organs and structures of animals.

whorl. One of the turns of a spiral shell.

zoöecium. The outer coverings of zoöids that give them their structural support.

zoöid. The polyp in bryozoans.

zoöphyte. An animal which resembles a plant.

REFERENCES

Arnold, Augusta F. 1968. *The Sea-Beach at Ebb-Tide.* New York: Dover Publications.

Barnes, Robert D. 1963. *Invertebrate Zoology.* Philadelphia: W. B. Saunders Company.

Department of Fisheries, State of Washington. 1976. *Pacific Northwest Marine Fishes.* Olympia: Washington State Printers.

Flora, Charles J. 1977. *The Sound and the Sea.* Olympia: The Washington State Department of Printing.

Friese, E. V. 1968. *Guide to the Point Defiance Aquarium.* Tacoma, Washington: Johnson Cox Company.

Furlong, Marjorie and Virginia Pill. 1973. *Starfish.* Tacoma, Washington: Erco, Inc.

Garl, G. C. 1971. *Some Common Marine Fishes of British Columbia.* Victoria, Canada: K. M. MacDonald, Queen's Printer.

Guberlet, Muriel L. 1962. *Animals of the Seashore.* Portland, Oregon: Binfords and Mort.

Hewlett, Stefanie. 1976. *Sea Life of the Pacific Northwest.* Toronto, Canada: McGraw Hill Ryerson Limited.

Johnson, M. E. and H. J. Snook. 1955. *Seashore Animals of the Pacific Coast.* New York: Dover Publishing Inc.

Kozloff, Eugene N. 1974. *Keys to the Marine Invertebrates of Puget Sound, the San Juan Archipelago, and Adjacent Regions.* Seattle: University of Washington Press.

——— . 1973. *Seashore Life of Puget Sound, the Strait of Georgia, and the San Juan Archipelago.* Seattle: University of Washington Press.

Meglitsch, Paul. 1972. *Invertebrate Zoology.* New York: Oxford University Press.

Palmer, E. Lawrence and Seymour H. Fowler. 1975. *Fieldbook of Natural History.* New York: McGraw Hill.

Rice, Tom. 1973. *Marine Shells of the Pacific Coast.* Tacoma, Washington: Erco, Inc.

Ricketts, Edward F. and Jack Calvin. 1969. *Between Pacific Tides.* Palo Alto: Stanford University Press.

Sherman, Irwin. 1970. *The Invertebrates: Function and Form, a Laboratory Guide.* New York: MacMillan Co.

Somerton, David and Craig Murray. 1976. *Field Guide to the Fish of Puget Sound and the Northwest Coast.* Seattle: University of Washington Press.

Storer, Tracy I. and Robert L. Usinger. 1957. *General Zoology.* New York: McGraw-Hill Book Company, Inc.

INDEX